THE RELIGIOUS LIFE OF INDIA

THE VILLAGE GODS OF SOUTH INDIA

THE RELIGIOUS LIFE OF INDIA

THE VILLAGE GODS OF SOUTH INDIA

BY THE

RIGHT REVEREND HENRY WHITEHEAD, D.D.
BISHOP OF MADRAS

SECOND EDITION, REVISED AND ENLARGED

GYAN

Published by

Gyan Publishing House
5, Ansari Road
Daryaganj, New Delhi-110002
Phone: 011-47034999, 9811692060
E-mail: books@gyanbooks.com

Distribution Network
gyanbooks.com
India, USA, Canada, UK, Australia, France

ISBN : 978-81-212-4187-8 (PB)
First Published, London, 1921

2nd Impression 2020

Printed at: Gyan Press, Delhi.

The Religious Life of India
The Village Gods of South India
Author: Right Reverend Henry Whitehead

THE RELIGIOUS LIFE OF INDIA

EDITED BY

J. N. FARQUHAR, M.A., D.Litt.,

LITERARY SECRETARY, NATIONAL COUNCIL, YOUNG MEN'S CHRISTIAN ASSOCIATIONS, INDIA, BURMA AND CEYLON;

AND

NICOL MACNICOL, M.A., D.Litt.

ALREADY PUBLISHED

THE AHMADĪYA MOVEMENT. By H. A. WALTER, M.A.

THE CHAMĀRS. By G. W. BRIGGS, M.Sc., Cawnpore.

UNDER PREPARATION

THE HINDU RELIGIOUS YEAR. By M. M. UNDERHILL, B.A., B.Litt., Nasik.

THE VAISHṆAVISM OF PANDHARPUR. By NICOL MACNICOL, M.A., D.Litt., Poona.

THE CHAITANYAS. By M. T. KENNEDY, M.A., Calcutta.

THE ŚRĪ-VAISHṆAVAS. By E. C. WORMAN, M.A., Madras.

THE RĀMĀNANDĪS. By C. T. GROVES, M.A., Fyzabad.

KABĪR AND HIS FOLLOWERS. By F. E. KEAY, M.A., Jubbulpore.

THE DĀDŪPANTHĪS. By W. G. ORR, M.A., B.D., Jaipur.

THE VĪRA ŚAIVAS. By W. E. TOMLINSON, Mangalore, and W. PERSTON, Tumkur.

THE TAMIL ŚAIVA SIDDHĀNTA. By GORDON MATTHEWS, M.A., B.D., Madras, and J. S. MASILAMANI, B.D., Pasumalai.

THE BRĀHMA MOVEMENT. By MANILAL C. PAREKH, B.A., Rajkot, Kathiawar.

THE RĀMAKṚISHṆA MOVEMENT. By J. N. C. GANGULY, B.A., Calcutta.

THE KHOJAS. By W. M. HUME, B.A., Lahore.

THE MĀLĀS AND MĀDIGĀS. By the BISHOP OF DORNAKAL, P. B. EMMET, B.A., Kurnool, and S. NICHOLSON, Cuddapah.

THE ḌHEDS. By MRS. SINCLAIR STEVENSON, M.A., Sc.D., Rajkot, Kathiawar.

THE MAHĀRS. By A. ROBERTSON, M.A., Poona.

THE BHILS. By D. LEWIS, Jhalod, Panch Mahals.

THE CRIMINAL TRIBES. By O. H. B. STARTE, I.C.S., Bijapur.

EDITORIAL PREFACE

THE purpose of this series of small volumes on the leading forms which religious life has taken in India is to produce really reliable information for the use of all who are seeking the welfare of India. Editor and writers alike desire to work in the spirit of the best modern science, looking only for the truth. But, while doing so and seeking to bring to the interpretation of the systems under review such imagination and sympathy as characterize the best study in the domain of religion to-day, they believe they are able to shed on their work fresh light drawn from the close religious intercourse which they have each had with the people who live by the faith herein described; and their study of the relevant literature has in every instance been largely supplemented by persistent questioning of those likely to be able to give information. In each case the religion described is brought into relation with Christianity. It is believed that all readers in India at least will recognize the value of this practical method of bringing out the salient features of Indian religious life.

THE RELIGIOUS LIFE OF INDIA

THE VILLAGE GODS OF SOUTH INDIA

BY THE

RIGHT REVEREND HENRY WHITEHEAD, D.D.,

BISHOP OF MADRAS

SECOND EDITION, REVISED AND ENLARGED

ASSOCIATION PRESS
(Y.M.C.A.)
5, RUSSELL STREET, CALCUTTA

HUMPHREY MILFORD
OXFORD UNIVERSITY PRESS
LONDON, NEW YORK, TORONTO, MELBOURNE, BOMBAY,
MADRAS AND CALCUTTA
1921

PREFACE

The material for this account of the village gods of South India has been gathered almost entirely from my own observation and inquiry. I have been able to get little help from books, as this is, I think, the first attempt at dealing systematically with this aspect of Indian religion. It does not pretend to be anything like an exhaustive account of all the various rites and ceremonies observed in the worship of the village deities. The variety of ritual and ceremonial in the different districts of South India is almost endless, and I have not attempted in this book to give an account even of all the various ceremonies that have come within my own knowledge. Perhaps it would be more correct to call the book "An Introduction to the Study of the Village Gods of South India." I believe, however, that all the main types of this particular form of Hinduism are included in the following pages, and that enough has been said to enable the reader to get a fairly complete idea of its general character and to compare it with similar forms of religion in other parts of the world.

I have to acknowledge the kindness of the Editor of *The Nineteenth Century and After* for allowing me to reprint in Chapters IV, VI, and VII portions of articles contributed by me to that Magazine. I owe the drawings from which illustrations have been made to Mrs. Whitehead; while Miss Stephen, the Archdeacon of Madras, and other friends have most kindly supplied me with the photographs used for that purpose; and the Government of Madras has generously allowed me to use the plates for some of the illustrations which previously appeared in a bulletin that I wrote some years ago for the Madras Museum.

A Glossary of Indian Terms and several Indices have been included in order to facilitate reference to the large amount of unfamiliar detail which the book contains.

HENRY MADRAS.

CONTENTS

ILLUSTRATIONS

INTRODUCTION

The worship of the village gods is the most ancient form of Indian religion. Before the Aryan invasion, which probably took place in the second millennium B.C., the old inhabitants of India, who are sometimes called Dravidians, were a dark-skinned race, with religious beliefs and customs that probably did not greatly differ from those of other primitive races. They believed the world to be peopled by a multitude of spirits, good and bad, who were the cause of all unusual events, and especially of diseases and disasters. The object of their religion was to propitiate these innumerable spirits. At the same time, each village seems to have been under the protection of some one spirit, who was its guardian deity. Probably these village deities came into being at the period when the people began to settle down in agricultural communities. We may see in them the germs of the national deities which were so prominent among the Semitic races and the great empires of Egypt, Nineveh, and Babylon. Where the family developed into a clan, and the clan into a tribe, and the tribe into a nation, and the nation into a conquering empire, the god of the family naturally developed into an imperial deity. But in ancient India, before the coming of the Aryans, the population seems to have been split up into small agricultural and pastoral communities. There were no nations and no conquering empires. And it was not till the Aryan invaders had conquered North India and had settled down in the country, that there was in India any growth of philosophic thought about the world as a whole. The problem of the universe did not interest the simple Dravidian folk. They only looked for an explanation of the facts and troubles of village life. Their religion, therefore, did not advance beyond a crude animism and belief in village deities. Later on, after the Aryans had overrun a large part of India, and the Brāhmans had established their ascendency as a priestly caste, the old Dravidian cults were influenced by the superior religion of the Aryans, and strongly reacted on them in turn.

The earliest Indian philosophical systems arose in the sixth century B.C., under the stimulus of the desire to escape from transmigration. Two of these developed into new religions hostile to Hinduism, namely Jainism and Buddhism, while others remained in the old faith. All exercised a profound influence on the thought of India and also modified religious practice in certain respects. On the other hand, the crude ideas and barbarous cults of the omnipresent aboriginal tribes, constantly pressing upon the life of the Aryans, found entrance into their religion at many points. Thus the old polytheistic nature-worship of the *Ṛigveda*, with its animal sacrifices offered in the open air, and its simple, healthy rules for family and social life, was gradually transformed into a great mass of warring sects holding philosophical ideas and subtle theological systems, and condemning animal sacrifice, yet worshipping gross idols, and bound by innumerable superstitions. Caste arose and became hardened into the most rigorous system of class distinctions that the world has ever seen, inspired and justified by the doctrine of transmigration and karma.

What we now call Hinduism, therefore, is a strange medley of the most diverse forms of religion, ranging from the most subtle and abstruse systems of philosophy to primitive forms of animism. At the same time, the primitive forms of Dravidian religion have been in their turn greatly modified by Brāhman influence. For the most part, the same people in town and village worship the village deities and the Brāhman gods. There are a few aboriginal tribes in some of the hill tracts who are still unaffected by Brāhman ideas or customs, but in the vast majority of the districts the worship of the village deities and the worship of Śiva and Vishṇu go on side by side; just as in China Confucianism and Taoism are not rival religions but complementary creeds.

To the student of comparative religion the study of the weird rites and ceremonies connected with the propitiation of the village deities is interesting, because it reveals many points of contact with primitive forms of religion in other lands, and also because it enables the student to see these primitive religious ideas in very different stages of development. To the Christian the study has a still greater interest, because, amid all their repulsive features, these rites contain instinctive ideas and yearnings which find their satisfaction in the highest truths of Christianity.

In the second edition I have tried to remedy defects and omissions that have been kindly pointed out by reviewers, and some chapters have been rearranged. It has been difficult, however, to know where to stop when attempting to supply omissions. The number of different gods and goddesses worshipped all over South India is enormous and the variety of local customs almost infinite. It is inevitable, therefore, that a large number of deities and customs, which are both interesting and important, should be omitted in a small book that can only aim at being a brief introduction to a vast subject.

The chapter on the probable origin of the worship of village gods (Ch. VIII) has naturally provoked the most criticism. In the former chapters I have stated what I have heard and seen myself. In this chapter I rashly entered the field of conjecture and framed a hypothesis as to what may have happened about 7000 years ago. Naturally I have laid myself open to attack. But in spite of the criticisms that have been made on my theory, I do not feel inclined to give it up, though it must necessarily remain incapable of proof. I am still of opinion that the totemistic theory of the origin of the sacrifices to the grāma-devatās, or village goddesses, as distinct from the offerings made to the spirits of ancestors or other deities, is on the whole most in accordance with the facts. Professor Elmore, in his able and most interesting book, *Dravidian Gods in Modern Hinduism*, criticizes the totemistic theory of the origin of the buffalo-sacrifice, which is the most important of the sacrifices offered to the grāma-devatās, on three grounds, mainly because the existing stories, current amongst the people, suggest a historical origin for the rites. Professor Elmore conjectures from these stories that the sacrifices symbolize "the dire punishment and disgrace of a conquered enemy." The cutting off of the head, the putting the foreleg in the mouth, the smearing of the nose with fat and the putting of a lighted lamp upon the forehead, are, in this theory, intended to express "the supreme humiliation of a feared, despised, and defeated enemy." So the procession of the buffalo with a garland round its neck, through the village before the sacrifice, is described as "the remnant of a triumphal procession in which the enemy was exhibited before the disgraceful death." The sacrifice, therefore, represents the triumph of the Aryan invaders over the Dravidian aborigines and their "mad gods."

I must confess that this explanation seems to me very far-fetched and improbable, and entirely out of line with all that we know about the origin and meaning of sacrifice and ritual among other peoples, and it is open to the fatal objection that it compels us to assume that these buffalo-sacrifices originated at a comparatively late date, long after the Aryan invasion of North India and subsequent to the advance of the Aryans into South India, when the struggle with the Dravidians was over and the triumph of the Aryans assured. The stories which I have given in Chapter VII, and those which Professor Elmore gives in his book to support his theory, obviously belong to the time when the Pariahs of South India, who were originally a leading clan among the Dravidians, had been dethroned from their position and reduced to a state of servitude and degradation by Brāhman influence. But it seems to me quite clear that the worship of the grāma-devatās and the buffalo-sacrifice belong to a very much older period than this, and go back to the days long before the Aryan invasion, probably to the time when the Dravidian clans first came to India and settled down to an agricultural life. If that is true, it is impossible to interpret the meaning of rites and ceremonies which originated about 3000 or 4000 B.C. at the latest, by the light of legends which represent historical events that took place about three thousand years later.

Again, in view of the facts that agricultural deities all over the world have been mainly female, and that many of the rites and ceremonies connected with the worship of the grāma-devatās are obviously related to the harvest, I must still maintain my opinion that the reason why the grāma-devatās are female is because they were originally agricultural deities. Professor Elmore's view, that the Dravidian deities are female because the Dravidian women were specially quarrelsome, vindictive and jealous, and that their tempers and curses made people feel that it was wise to propitiate female spirits, seems to me a very improbable explanation, even if it were certain that Dravidian women were as much "adepts in the use of bad languages and vigorous terms of defamation" six thousand years ago as some of them are to-day.

CHAPTER I

LEADING FEATURES OF THE RELIGION

THE worship of the Village Deity, or *grāma-devatā*, as it is called in Sanskrit and in Tamil, forms an important part of the conglomerate of religious beliefs, customs, and ceremonies which are generally classed together under the term Hinduism. In almost every village and town of South India may be seen a shrine or symbol of the grāma-devatā, and in every village the grāma-devatā is periodically worshipped and propitiated. As a rule this shrine is far less imposing than the Brāhmanical temples in the neighbourhood; very often it is nothing more than a small brick building three are four feet high, or a small enclosure with a few rough stones in the centre; and often there is no shrine at all; but still, when calamity overtakes the village, when pestilence or famine or cattle disease makes its appearance, it is to the village deity that the whole body of the villagers turn for protection. Śiva and Vishṇu may be more dignified beings, but the village deity is regarded as a more present help in trouble, and is more intimately concerned with the happiness and prosperity of the villagers.

(*a*) *The origin* of this form of Hinduism is lost in antiquity; but it is certain that it represents a pre-Aryan cult of the Dravidian peoples, more or less modified in various parts of South India by Brāhmanical influence; and some details of the ceremonies seem to point back to a totemistic stage of religion. The normal function of the grāma-devatā is the guardianship of the village, but many of them are believed to have other powers, especially in relation to disease and calamity.

(*b*) The village deities and their worship are *widely different from the popular Hindu deities*, Śiva and Vishṇu, and the worship that centres in the great Hindu temples.

1. Śiva and Vishṇu represent forces of nature: Śiva symbolizes the power of destruction and the idea of life through death, Vishṇu the power of preservation and the idea of salvation. Both these deities and the system of religion connected with them are the outcome of philosophic reflection on the universe as a whole. But the village deities, on the other hand, have no relation to the universe. *They symbolize only the facts of village life.* They are related, not to great world forces, but to such simple facts as cholera, small-pox, and cattle disease.

2. Then, in the second place, *village deities*, with very few exceptions, *are female.* Śiva and Vishṇu, and the principal deities of the Hindu pantheon, are male. Their wives, it is true, play an important part in Hindu religious life—Kālī especially, the "black one," the wife of Śiva, is the presiding deity of Calcutta, and is one of the chief deities of Bengal—but, speaking generally, in the Hindu pantheon the male deities are predominant and the female deities occupy a subordinate position. This is characteristic of the genius of the Aryan religion, but in the old Dravidian cults a leading feature was the worship of the female principle in nature. It is possible that this is due to the fact that the Aryan deities were the gods of a race of warriors, whereas the Dravidian deities were the goddesses of an agricultural people. All over the world, the gods of war are mostly male, while the agricultural deities are, for the most part, female; and this naturally arises from the fact that war is the business of men, whereas, among primitive peoples, the cultivation of the fields was largely left to the women, and also from the fact that the idea of fertility is naturally connected with the female. All over Southern India, therefore, the

village deities are almost exclusively female. In the Tamil country, it is true, most of them have male attendants, who are supposed to guard the shrines and carry out the commands of the goddesses; but their place is distinctly subordinate and almost servile. One of these male deities, however, Iyenar, has an independent position. He generally has a shrine to himself, and is regarded as the night-watchman of the village. The compound of his shrine is generally crowded with clay figures of horses, great and small, on which he is supposed to ride round the village during the watches of the night, to keep off evil spirits. In the Telugu country, too, there is a being called Potu-Razu, who figures sometimes as the brother, sometimes as the husband, of the village goddess, and sometimes as merely an attendant; but I have never met him as an independent deity and have always been told that sacrifice is never offered to him alone, but only in conjunction with one or more of the goddesses.

3. Then, in the third place, the village deities are almost universally *worshipped with animal sacrifices.* Buffaloes, sheep, goats, pigs, and fowls are freely offered to them, sometimes in thousands. In the Tamil country, this custom is curiously modified by the influence of Brāhmanism, which has imbued the villagers with the idea that the shedding of blood is low and irreligious, and it is remarkable that no animal sacrifices are ever offered to Iyenar. The male attendants accept them eagerly, and take toddy and cheroots into the bargain; but Iyenar is regarded as far too good a being to be pleased by the sight of bloodshed.

4. Again, the *pūjārīs, i.e. the priestly ministrants,* the men who perform the *pūjā, i.e. the worship, are not Brāhmans,*[1] but are drawn from all the other castes.

[1] The whole Hindu people in North India may be likened to a great step-pyramid, consisting of five stories. These are exclusive groups, marked off from each other by deep distinctions in religious and social standing and in ideal function :

It is hardly ever possible to make any general statement about any subject in India without at once being confronted with facts which seem to prove that you are wrong; accordingly, I may mention that I have found cases where Brāhmans officiate as pūjārīs at the shrines of village deities. I came across one such case at Negapatam; while, at Bangalore, I actually found a case where a Brāhman widow was the ministrant. About three miles from Tanjore, too, there is a temple of Mariamma served by Brāhman priests. But no animal sacrifices are offered at the central shrine where Brāhmans minister. In one corner of the temple area there is a separate shrine with an image of Mariamma where animals are regularly sacrificed; but at this shrine no Brāhmans officiate. I believe that it is the only temple or shrine of Mariamma in South India where there are Brāhman priests. But then, in these cases the Brāhman pūjārī never has anything to do with animal sacrifices. These are always conducted entirely by men of lower castes, and, even so, it is a degradation for a Brāhman to be connected as pūjārī with a shrine where such abominations take place; but, according to the Indian proverb, "For the sake of one's stomach one must play many parts." Setting aside these exceptional cases, it may be stated generally that no

Brāhmans: priests Kshatriyas: kings and warriors Vaiśyas: farmers and tradesmen	In North India these three groups are held to be of pure Aryan blood and called twice-born.
Śūdras: servants	Aboriginals, reckoned pure and admitted to the temples.
Outcastes, Pañchamas (*i.e.* fifth-class men)	Unclean, untouchable aboriginals.

Foreigners are held unclean, and are called *mlecchas*. In South India, it is to be noticed, the farmers, artisans, and tradesmen are all classed as Śūdras, and the Kshatriyas are practically non-existent. The population, therefore, is divided into three main groups: the Brāhmans of Aryan blood; the Śūdras, who are Dravidians, admitted to the temples; and the Outcastes, who are partly Dravidians and partly still older inhabitants, not admitted to the temples.

Brāhmans are the priests of village deities, but that the pūjārīs are drawn from all other castes indiscriminately, while an important part in the worship, especially that connected with the buffalo-sacrifices, is even taken by Outcastes. As will be seen later on, the buffalo-sacrifice has special features of its own, and seems to retain traces of a primitive form of worship, which may possibly have originated in totemism.

In addition to the grāma-devatās, who are in a special sense the village deities, there are a large number of spirits of all kinds, male and female, who are worshipped by the villagers. The worship of departed ancestors played an important part in the old Dravidian religion and is still universal all over South India. So men and women, boys and girls, who have died violent or untimely deaths, or who have been notorious for their power or even their crimes, are frequently worshipped after death. It is probable that a large proportion of these gods have been reverenced for centuries, but many are of quite recent origin. Some were originally people who were murdered, or who during their lifetime were feared for their power or their crimes, or women who died in child-birth. It is easy to observe a deity in the making even at the present day.

A district superintendent of police in the Telugu country told me that in 1904, at a village some twelve miles from Ellore, two little boys, minding cattle in the fields, thought they heard the sound of trumpets proceeding from an ant-hill. They told the story in the village, and at once the people turned out and did pūjā to the deity in the ant-hill. The fame of the deity's presence spread like wild-fire far and wide, and the village became the centre of pilgrimages from all the country round about. Every Sunday as many as 5,000 people, men and women, assembled before the ant-hill, and might be seen prostrate on their faces, rapt in adoration. The incident illustrates the ease with which a local cult springs up in India and suddenly becomes popular over a large district.

Another instance came to my notice a few years ago at Bezwada. A small boy, the son of well-to-do parents, was murdered near the town for the sake of his ornaments, and thrown into the canal. The body was discovered and placed under a tree near the bank of the canal, at a place where three roads meet. A little after, a small shrine, about a foot and a half high, was built by the parents under a tree to the spirit of the murdered boy. Then some one declared that he had made a vow at the shrine and obtained his desire. The fame of the shrine at once spread, the spirit of the boy rose quite to the rank of a minor deity, and a local worship speedily sprang up and became popular. When I last saw the shrine it had been enlarged and had become about twice its original size.

About sixty years ago a Hindu widow, named Rāmamma, lived between Bezwada and Hyderabad, farming some land left her by her husband. After a time she contracted immoral relations with one of her servants, Buddha Sahib. Her brother was so angry that he murdered them both. Then the cattle-plague broke out; and the villagers connected it with the wrath of the murdered Rāmamma, and instituted special rites to pacify her spirit. And now, whenever there is cattle-plague in the district, two rough wooden images, about two feet high, are made to represent Maddha Rāmamma and Buddha Sahib, and, with two images of local goddesses as their attendants, are put on a small wooden cart and dragged in procession at night round all the principal streets of the village, accompanied by fireworks, music, and *nautch-girls* (*i.e.* dancing-girls of loose character connected with Hindu temples). Finally, the cart is dragged to the boundary of the village lands and thrown into the territory of the adjacent village, in order to transfer to it the angry spirit of Rāmamma.

Temples have been built to Plague-amma during the last ten years, as a result of the prevalence of plague.

Special reverence is paid to persons who come to

an untimely end, *e.g.* to the spirits of girls who die before marriage, but when the circumstances of their death specially strikes the imagination of the general public, the reverence which is ordinarily confined to the family expands into a regular local cult.

Then, again, there is the spirit of the boundary stone, the spirits of hills and rivers, forests and trees, the deities of particular arts and crafts, who are worshipped by particular classes of the population. The worship of serpents, especially the deadly cobra, is common all over South India. In one village of the Wynaad I came across a Mission school which was visited almost daily by a large cobra, which glided undisturbed and harmless through the school-room. Neither teachers nor pupils would have dared to kill it. Constantly they fed it with milk. In many towns and villages large slabs of stone with figures of cobras, often two cobras intertwined, carved in bas-relief are seen on a platform under a large tree. They are worshipped especially by women who want children.

CHAPTER II

NAMES, CHARACTERS, AND FUNCTIONS OF THE VILLAGE GODS

(*a*) THE *names* of village deities are legion. Some of them have an obvious meaning, many are quite unintelligible to the people themselves, and I have often failed to get any clue to their origin, even from native paṇḍits. They differ in almost every district, and often the deities worshipped in one village will be quite unknown in other villages five or six miles off. In Masulipatam on the East Coast, in the Telugu country, the following were given me as the names of the village deities worshipped in the district, *viz*. Mutyalamma, the pearl goddess (*amma* or *amman* is only a female termination); Chinnintamma, the goddess who is head of the house; Challalamma, the goddess presiding over buttermilk; Ghantalamma, the goddess who goes with bells; Yaparamma, the goddess who transacts business; Mamillamma, the goddess who sits under a mango tree; Gaṅgamma, the water goddess, who in this district is the protectress against small-pox.

But, at a village about twenty miles from Masulipatam, I found that fifteen different goddesses were worshipped in the neighbourhood, of whom only four were identical with those of Masulipatam. Some were named after the villages from which they had been imported, *e.g.* Addankamma, the goddess from Addanki, and Pandilamma, the goddess from Pandil; others had names derived from common objects of country life, *e.g.* Wanamalamma, the goddess of the tope, Balamma, the goddess of the cart, and Śītalamma, the water goddess.

In the Ellore district, farther west, the deities

worshipped are chiefly Gaṅgamma, who is sometimes called Mahālakshmī (one of the names of Vishṇu's wife), and sometimes Chamalamma (another name of Kālī, the wife of Śiva), and Poleramma, the boundary goddess, and Aṅkamma, who is regarded as the goddess of cholera and disease generally.

Farther west than Ellore, across the hills, in the Cuddapah and Kurnool districts, the village goddess is often known simply as Peddamma (great goddess) or Chinnamma (little goddess). In many villages, however, of these districts these names are unknown, and the village deities are called Gaṅgamma, Polamma, and Suṅkalamma, etc. In some villages the village deities consist of Potu-Razu and his seven sisters, who are known by various names. In one village they were given me as Peddamma, Isondamma, Maramma, Aṅkalamma, Nukalamma, Vasukota, Ellamma, and Arikamma.

Again, Kālīamma or Kālī is said to be the only one of the village goddesses whose name is found in the Vedas. She is an *avatāra*, or incarnation of the eight powers of the universe. The story told about her is that a demon named Mahishāsura (the buffalo demon) gave great offence to Śiva, and was condemned to death. But, owing to a privilege bestowed on him by Śiva himself, he could not be slain by the Trimūrti[1] nor by any male deity. So the task was given to Kālī, who successfully accomplished it, and so won a place among village deities.

At Cuddalore I visited a shrine of the goddess Mīnāchīamman at the village of Devanampatnam. It stands on the seashore on a low ridge of sand. There is no building, but an oblong space about 20 by 12 feet is enclosed on three sides by rows of clay figures, the eastern end towards the sea being left open. On the western side of the oblong, facing the sea, there were

[1] This word is used for an image with three heads, representing Brahmā, Vishṇu, and Śiva as a triple manifestation of the divine nature.

two small clay figures, apparently a man and a woman, seated in the centre. They were about a foot high with the remains of old garlands on them. To the left and right of them were figures of seven virgins (or Saptakannigais), very well modelled in clay and about nine inches high. In front of them and beside them were the figures of male guardians and attendants. On each side of the images of the virgins was a figure of a large round fish, with open mouth and staring eyes, and seated on the back of each fish were the figures of a man and a woman. The pūjārī of the shrine told me that the woman was Mīnāchī the fish-goddess, and the man Madurai-Vīran. Beside each fish were figures of guardians and attendants. The north and south sides of the oblong, which are about twenty-one feet in length, are formed by clay figures of horses and elephants, some of them with men on their backs. The elephants are quaint creatures, very like horses with trunks. The horses are not in this case steeds of the god Iyenar, but simply the attendants of Mīnāchī and the seven virgins. Animal sacrifices, consisting of goats, cocks, etc., are offered to these deities once a year at an annual festival. The people at the shrine gave the name of the fish as something like ullai; but the translator of the district and sessions court of South Arcot told me that the fish on which Mīnāchī and Madurai-Vīran are seated is the ullan fish, which is a sea-fish that runs up the river in flood-times, when the bar is open, and generally travels a considerable distance till it meets with an anicut or some similar obstacle. It gets very fat and is a favourite dish. The goddess Mīnāchī, who is seated on it, is commonly worshipped by fishermen, who swear by her name. She is the goddess worshipped in the great temple of Madura together with the god Śiva. Madurai-Vīran is a male attendant of nearly all the village goddesses throughout the Tamil country, and he is generally represented by a small conical stone or the image of a man carved in bas-relief on a stone slab, standing outside the shrine.

The Saptakannigais (the seven virgins), or Akasakannigais (the heavenly virgins), are the tutelary deities of tanks, and the figures of the Kannigais seated in a row are often carved on a small stone and placed on tank bunds, especially at places where the tank has been breached. In the North Arcot district they are described as female creatures who are very quarrelsome, and, when they fight, breaches are caused in the tanks by the stamping of their feet. At the same time they are supposed to protect tanks, and when the flood rises to a dangerous point, it is said that one of the Kannigais, in the shape of a little child, runs through the village knocking at the doors and calling up the villagers to come and protect the bund. It is believed that people walking alone along a tank bund have sometimes met the Saptakannigais, going in procession with horses and torches, and that any one who sees them invariably dies. The district judge told me that, in a case which came before him in the North Arcot district, a man who really died by a fracture of his skull, because a cousin of his had hit him on the head with a thick sugarcane, was reported to have died as the result of meeting a procession of the Saptakannigais on the tank bund, and that the village magistrate excused himself for not reporting the man's death, because he considered it to be a death by natural causes.

A male deity, called Kuttandavar, is worshipped in many parts of the Tamil country, especially in the South Arcot district. At the village of Devanampatnam, near Cuddalore, I saw an image of this god in a small shrine built of brick, with a rough pandal of bamboos, thatched with cocoanut leaves, in front of it. The image consisted of a head, like a big mask, about three feet high, with a rubicund face, strong features, moustaches turning up at the end, lion's teeth projecting downwards outside the mouth from the angles of the upper jaw, and a tall conical head-dress, called in Tamil *Krittam*. Below this stone there was a small stone head about one and a half feet high, which was a miniature of the larger figure, It was finely chiselled and the people told me that it was the work of the stone-masons who made the new images of Tirupapuliyur temple. Both images had the mark of Vishṇu on their foreheads, so also had the pūjārī of the shrine. The pūjārī said that the images represented the god Kuttandavar, and he told me the following legend about him. The god Indra, for the crime of murdering a Brāhman, became incarnated in the form of Kuttandavar, and a curse was laid upon him that his body should rot away, leaving only the head; with the result that no one would give him his daughter in marriage; because, if they were married in the morning, his body would rot away before the evening and so the bride would become a widow and the *tali* be cut. Śrī Kṛishṇa, however, took pity on him, assumed the female form of Mohinī, and consented to be married to him in the morning, and then, as he vanished all but the head, the *tali* was cut in the evening. In memory of this event, during the festival, which is celebrated in the month of *Chitrai* (April), a crowd of men dressed as women come to the shrine with *talis* on their necks. In the evening at sunset the *tali* is cut, because the god has died and all the people dressed as women have become widows. The festival, therefore, is necessarily limited to the day-time. Fowls and goats are sacrificed to the god a little distance in front of the shrine. The festival is attended by all non-Brāhman castes. The people who showed me the shrines said that Kuttandavar is so named from an Asura, or Demon or Kuttu, whom the god killed. But as Kuttandavar is especially the god of the actors or dancers, or *Kuttadis*, who are very numerous in South Arcot and are a sub-division of the Padaiyachi caste, it seems likely that the name is derived from *Kuttadi* (a dancer or actor). I was told that wherever the Vaniyars or Padaiyachis are in great numbers, for instance, in the South Arcot, Coimbatore and Salem districts, and in the city of Madras, one is sure to see a large number of shrines of the god Kuttandavar. The worship of this god is, however, not considered to be very respectable. There is apparently no immorality connected with his worship, but more respectable members of the caste do not like men dressing like women. The members of the Padaiyachi caste, therefore, who have been educated in recent years and have risen in the social scale, tend to give up the worship of Kuttandavar.

I have often seen on the seashore of Madras a conical heap of sand, about three inches high, standing on a small platform of sand, with camphor and incense in a small earthenware vessel or in a heap of old netting. The conical heap of sand represents the goddess Kanniamma, the grāma-devatā of the fishing village. The fishermen have told me that she is the goddess who gives them fish and enables them to make a living, and that they make these offerings to her when fish are scarce and they have reason to think that she is angry. This illustrates the characteristic feature of all animistic worship. Its chief if not only motive is to propitiate the angry deity. Probably something of the same feeling lurks beneath the custom of Roman Catholic fishermen, when they bring holy water from the church and sprinkle it on their nets after they have toiled all the day and caught nothing. Probably the object of this custom is to exorcise a malignant spirit from the nets.

In the Mysore country I came across quite a different set of names for the village goddesses. At one village, near Bangalore, the name of the goddess was Maheśvaramma (great goddess), also called Savaramma (she who rides on horseback). Her sister, Doddamma, and her brother, Muneśvara, share in the worship paid to her. At another village a goddess, called Pūjamma (she who is worshipped), was shown to me. She was said to be the local goddess of the *Mādigās*, the lowest section of the Outcastes in the Telugu country; but at the same time the Śūdras[1] make vows to her, to induce her to ward off diseases from their homes, and then fulfil their vows by sacrificing buffaloes or thrusting

[1] See note on p. 19 above.

silver pins through their cheeks. Annamma is the principal goddess at another shrine in Bangalore City, and in the same shrine are six other deities, Chandeśvaramma, Māyeśvaramma, Maramma (the cholera goddess), Udalamma (she of the swollen neck), Kokkalamma (the goddess of coughs), Sukhajamma (the goddess of measles and small-pox).

At some villages a little distance from Bangalore the deity was simply the grāma-devatā, the village goddess. In Mysore City the grāma-devatā is know as Bisal-Mariamma (Bisal in Canarese means sunlight, and I was told that *Mari* means *śakti*[1] or power). The deity seems to have been originally connected with sun-worship. I was told that her shrines are never covered with a roof, and one of the symbols representing the deity is a brass pot full of water with a small mirror leaning against it, called *Kunna-Kannadi*, *i.e.* eye-mirror.

There are seven Mari deities, all sisters, who are worshipped in Mysore. All the seven sisters are regarded vaguely as wives or sisters of Śiva.

In Mysore villages Mahādeva-Amma, the great goddess, and Huliamma, the tiger-goddess, are found; and doubtless there are countless other names in the Mysore State for the many deities who are worshipped as the guardians of the villages and the averters of epidemics and other misfortunes.

It is quite probable that, originally, in South India the village goddesses had all quite simple names, such as Uramma or Grāma-devatā, both meaning village goddess, or Peddamma, great mother, and that the imagination of the villagers gradually invented special titles for their own guardian deities. But at the present time the village deities consist of a most miscellaneous collection of spirits, good, bad, and indifferent, who

[1] The chief Hindu gods are held to be actionless, far withdrawn from the bustle of the universe. In each case, however, the god's energy manifests itself in his wife, who is called his *śakti*. Those Hindus who worship Kālī, the wife of Śiva, are called *śāktas*. For *Māri* see also p. 32.

baffle all attempt at classification, enumeration, or explanation. A few of them, like Mariamma and Iyenar, have won their way to general respect or fear among the Tamil people; and, where Brāhman influence is strong, there has been an obvious attempt, as we have seen, to connect the village goddesses with the popular worship of Śiva or Vishṇu; but it is more than doubtful whether, originally, they had anything to do with either Śaivism or Vaishṇavism. The stories told about them in the folklore of the people, which represent them as *avatāras*, *i.e.* incarnations of Śiva, were probably quite late inventions, to account for names and ceremonies whose meaning had long been lost.

(*b*) The *characters* of the goddesses vary considerably. The villagers do not regard them as evil spirits, but neither do they regard them as unmixed benefactors. They are rather looked upon as beings of uncertain temper, very human in their liability to take offence. At Cocanada the pūjārīs told me that the village goddess, who is significantly called Nukalamma from a colloquial Tamil word meaning "to beat," causes all sorts of trouble and is dreaded as an evil spirit. But when an epidemic of cholera breaks out, they, curiously enough, install another goddess, called Maridiamma, in her place, and offer sacrifices to her instead of to Nukalamma, a proceeding calculated, one would have thought, to give dire offence.

Mahākālī, *i.e.* great Kālī, is another form or avatāra of the same goddess. She is supposed to be a deity of furious temper, and to be the cause of the prevalence of cholera. She is also known as Vīra-Mahākālī[1] or Ugra-Mahākālī,[2] to denote her rage and fury.

Another deity of similarly violent temper is Aṅgalamma, who is worshipped largely in the Coimbatore district. The idea seems to be that all who worship the *Ashṭa Śakti*, or eight powers of the

[1] Vīra is a Sanskrit word meaning heroic.
[2] Ugra is a Sanskrit word meaning fierce.

universe, will attain to bliss, while the others will be destroyed by Aṅgalamma. The people worship her to avoid falling victims to her unquenchable anger, since her main object is believed to be to devour and consume everything that comes in her way. She is said especially to have a great relish for bones!

Another deity of a very different disposition is Kāmāchīamma,[1] whose name implies that she is full of good and gracious qualities. She is reported to have been born a Brāhman girl, and then to have become the avatāra of one of the Ashṭa Śakti.

Another benevolent deity is Thuropathīamma, who is reported to have been the wife of a Ṛishi and a very virtuous woman; so, in her next birth, she was allowed to be born a king's daughter. Accordingly when Thurupatham, King of Pañchāla, offered a *puthrayāgam* (putrayāga, *i.e.* a sacrifice to obtain a child) she came forth from the fire. She afterwards became the wife of the Pāṇḍavas, the five brothers famous in the great Hindu epic, the *Mahābhārata*, and is regarded as one of the Ashṭa Śakti.

(*c*) The *functions* of the different goddesses are not at all clearly marked in the Telugu country. The people often told me "They are only different names for the same goddess." In some places there is a special cholera goddess, *e.g.* Aṅkamma, and in others a special small-pox goddess, *e.g.* Gaṅgamma; but as a rule the infliction and removal of epidemics and disasters is a general function of all goddesses alike. On the other hand, in the Coimbatore, Tanjore, and Trichinopoly districts of the Tamil country, where the people have been for many generations past far more influenced by civilization and Brāhmanism than in the Telugu country, I found that the functions of different deities were far more differentiated and that often elaborate stories were current as to their origin and characters. For example, one of the deities worshipped in almost

[1] Sanskrit Kāmākshī, "the love-eyed one," an epithet of Kālī, the wife of Śiva.

every village in the Tamil country is Mariamma or Māri, the goddess of small-pox.

It is noticeable that Mariamma is not found in any temples dedicated to one of the seven sisters, as she is considered superior to them in power and much worse in temper. The seven sisters are supposed to be kind and indulgent, while Mariamma is vindictive and inexorable and difficult to propitiate. The boundary goddess is worshipped in the Tanjore district under the name of Kālī, and her special function is to prevent any evil coming from without into the village of which she is the guardian, while the seven sisters are supposed to guard against any evil arising within the village itself. Though Mariamma keeps herself aloof from the seven sisters, I came across, in the South Arcot district, a shrine dedicated to Kanniamma (who was said to be another form of Mariamma and to preside over small-pox), in which were clay images of seven brothers. The youngest, called Muni (ghost), was the tallest and was represented by a larger clay figure seated on a raised platform, with his six smaller brothers standing beside him.

In the Tamil districts of Tanjore, Trichinopoly and Cuddalore, the names of village deities most commonly met with are Pidāri, which is often used as a generic name of village deities, Mariamma, Kālī, Seliamma, Draupati,[1] and Aṅgalamma. Mariamma is the commonest of them all, and her function is always to inflict or ward off small-pox. Pidāri is supposed to act as guardian against evil spirits and epidemics, especially cholera. Kālī is often regarded as especially the protectress against evil spirits that haunt forests and desolate places, and against wild beasts. In some parts she is the special goddess of the bird-catchers. But in some villages she is also the guardian against cholera. Except, however, in the villages near Tanjore, I have not met with Kālī in the capacity of a boundary goddess. In other places there are curious ceremonies

[1] This is for Draupadī, the heroine of the *Mahābhārata*.

connected with the boundary-stone, *ellai-kal* as it is called, and I was told in one village that in the boundary-stone reside evil spirits, which it is the object of the ceremonies to propitiate. In another village I found that there was a festival to a goddess called Ellai-Pidāri.[1]

(*d*) *Male deities.* Next to Mariamma, the deity that is most universally worshipped among the Tamils is Iyenar, and, as already stated, he is the one village deity, largely worshipped in the Tamil country, who seems to be an exception to the general rule that the village deities are female. In almost every Tamil village there is a shrine of Iyenar, who is regarded as the watchman of the village, and is supposed to patrol it every night, mounted on a ghostly steed, a terrible sight to behold, scaring away the evil spirits. He has always a separate shrine, and is not, like Munadian and Madurai-Vīran,[2] simply an attendant of a local goddess. His shrine may be known by the clay or concrete figures of horses ranged on either side of the image or piled about in the compound of the shrine in admired confusion. The horses are offered by devotees, and represent the steeds on which he rides in his nightly rounds. He is regarded by the villagers as a good and benevolent protector, of far higher character than the disreputable Madurai-Vīran.

Another male deity, of much inferior character to Iyenar, who is sometimes worshipped separately, is Karuppanna. As a rule he is simply one of the subordinate male attendants of the village goddess: but in some places I have met with separate shrines to Karuppanna, where he presides as the chief deity. At one of these shrines worship was offered exclusively by *Pariahs*.[3] At another place the evil spirit residing in the boundary-stone was called Ellai-Karuppu.

In one village in the Trichinopoly district, I came

[1] See below and cf. p. 101.
[2] Vīran is the Tamil form of *Vīra*, hero.
[3] The chief group of Outcastes in the Tamil country.

across a male deity known as Rāja Vayan (King Father), who was represented by four or five stakes, about five or six feet high, with iron spear-heads on top. The spears were stuck on one side of a stone platform under a tamarind and an areca tree, and reminded me of the wooden stakes representing Potu-Razu in the Telugu country. In one shrine belonging exclusively to the Pariahs of a village, I found that the chief deities were all male and not female. Whether these independent and semi-independent male deities have in all cases developed out of the subordinate male attendants of the village deities, or whether they belong to another Dravidian cult, it is difficult to say.

PLATE I

TYPICAL SHRINE OF GRĀMA-DEVATĀ

INTERIOR OF SHRINE WITH STONES AS SYMBOLS

PLATE II

TYPICAL SHRINE OF GRĀMA-DEVATĀ

CLAY HORSES OF IYENAR

CHAPTER III

THE CULT

Shrines, Symbols, Ministrants, Festivals

Shrines. The shrines of the village deities, destitute of uniformity or comeliness, are characteristic of this whole system of religion. They represent the dwelling-places of petty local deities concerned with the affairs of a petty local community. They express the meanness of a religion of fear. There is nothing about them to suggest feelings of adoration or love. Some of the shrines, especially in the Tamil country, are fairly large buildings, ornamented with grotesque figures, almost rivalling in size and architectural features the local temples of Śiva and Vishṇu. The shrines of Iyenar are distinguished by figures of horses great and small, on which he is supposed to ride round the village every night to chase away the evil spirits. But the majority of the shrines are mean little brick buildings of various shapes and sizes, often no more than four or five feet high, with a rough figure of the deity inside, carved in bas-relief on a small stone. In many villages the shrine is simply a rough stone platform under a tree, with stones or iron spears stuck on it to represent the deity. Often a large rough stone with no carving on it is stuck up in a field or under a tree, and serves for shrine and image alike. The boundary-stone of the village lands is very commonly regarded as a habitation of a local deity, and might be called a shrine or symbol with equal propriety.[1] In many villages of

[1] See above, p. 33.

the Telugu country there is no permanent shrine at all, but a temporary one is put up made of bamboo and cloth to accommodate the deity whenever a festival is held. It seems probable that this "tent of meeting" represents the primitive use, and that the permanent shrine was a later development, when individual worshippers began to make offerings in times of domestic trouble, and when the village community as a whole realized more fully the need of help and protection in the ordinary affairs of daily life.

Symbols. The images or symbols, by which the village deities are represented, are almost as diverse as their names. In some of the more primitive villages there is no permanent image or symbol of the deity at all; but a clay figure of the goddess is made by the potter, or the goldsmith, for each festival and then cast away beyond the boundaries of the village when the festival is ended. In other villages the deity is represented simply by a stone pillar standing in a field, or on a stone platform under a tree, or in a small enclosure surrounded by a stone wall. Often the stones, which represent the different deities, are simply small conical stones not more than five or six inches high, blackened with the anointing oil. It is difficult to see anything at all peculiar in them which in any way fits them to be symbols of the goddesses or their male attendants. In more civilized parts a slab of stone has the figure of a woman roughly carved upon it, sometimes with four, six, or eight arms, holding various implements in her hands, sometimes with only two arms, and sometimes with none at all.

Here is the description of a typical image which I saw in the Trichinopoly district. It was a stone figure of a woman, about two and a half feet high, with eight arms, and in her hands a knife, a shield, a bell, a devil's head, a drum, a three-pronged fork, a goad, and a piece of rope:[1] truly a collection of articles worthy of a schoolboy's pocket! Another image of the goddess

[1] Most of these objects appear in the hands of images of Śiva or of his wife Kālī.

made of the five metals (gold, silver, brass, copper, and lead) was kept, strangely enough, in the temple of Śiva, about two hundred yards off, for use in processions. It is very common in the Tamil districts to find a stone image fixed in the shrine, and a small portable metal image, which is used in processions during the festival.[1]

Very often, too, the goddess is represented in processions by a brass pot filled with water and decorated with margosa[2] leaves. I saw one of these brass pots in a shrine of Kālīamma at Shiyali, in the Tanjore district. It was about a foot high and a foot in diameter at the base, and had four tubes sticking out just below the neck. In other Tamil villages, where the image is fixed in the shrine and there is no metal image to carry in procession, an earthenware pot is used, filled with water and decorated with margosa leaves.

At Irungalur, in the Trichinopoly district, I found a small enclosure sacred to Kurumbaiamma, outside the village, without any image or sacred stones in it at all, and I was told that during the festival a small *pandal* (*i.e.* booth) of leaves is erected in the enclosure, under which a small earthen pot, curiously decorated, is placed to represent the goddess. The pot is filled with water, and has a silver two-anna piece (2d.) put inside it. Some cocoanut and oleander flowers are stuck in the mouth of the pot, surrounded and concealed by a sheaf of mango leaves, tied together by tender shoots of the banana tree. This bunch of mango leaves is then decorated with flowers, a small pointed stick of bamboo, with a lime stuck on the end, is inserted at the top of the bunch, and by the side of the lime a small silver umbrella with a silver handle. The decoration varies locally. This decorated pot is placed on a small platform of sand, and about eight measures of rice are heaped round the base of it. It is called *karagam*, *i.e.* the pot, and is carefully prepared at the chief local shrine of Kurumbaiamma,

[1] This practice is borrowed from Hindu temples.

[2] The margosa or neem tree is an evergreen bearing white flowers, *Melia Azadirachta*, and is frequently associated with village divinities.

about a mile outside the village, and during the festival is treated exactly like the goddess. It is taken round in procession on the head of a pūjārī to the sound of tom-toms[1] and pipes; offerings of fruit and flowers are made to it; a lamb is sacrificed before it, and it is worshipped with the orthodox prostrations.

The use made of the karagam is also worth notice. The following is from an article by Mr. F. J. Richards, I.C.S.:—

"The cholera goddess is popularly believed to be the mother of the washerman. He is therefore chosen to officiate as the pūjārī, as the son alone can hope to succeed in propitiating such a fierce divinity.

"A karagam is prepared; and the village washerman bathes early in the morning and places it on his head. Then, holding a sickle in one hand and margosa leaves in the other, he goes through the village dancing. Before the karagam procession takes place, all the villagers pour large quantities of ragi gruel into the big iron buckets used for baling water. When two or three of such buckets are filled, the poor people of the village are fed. The washerman dances at the place where the food is distributed. After dusk, when the procession passes through the village, sheep are sacrificed at the important centres in the village, and the blood collected in a mud vessel. The washerman, with the karagam on his head, goes on dancing through the limits of the village, preceded by the village musicians. At the point where his village borders on the adjoining village he places the karagam and the blood which had been collected at the different places of sacrifice, and returns home after taking a bath on his way. The goddess is believed to be propitiated by this, and any further attacks of cholera are attributed to the perfunctory discharge of this duty by the washerman. The sacrificial victims are sheep only, and the method of sacrifice is decapitation. The deity is thus propitiated and

[1] A tom-tom is a native drum. It is usually shaped like a small barrel, and beaten at both ends with the hands and fingers.

PLATE III

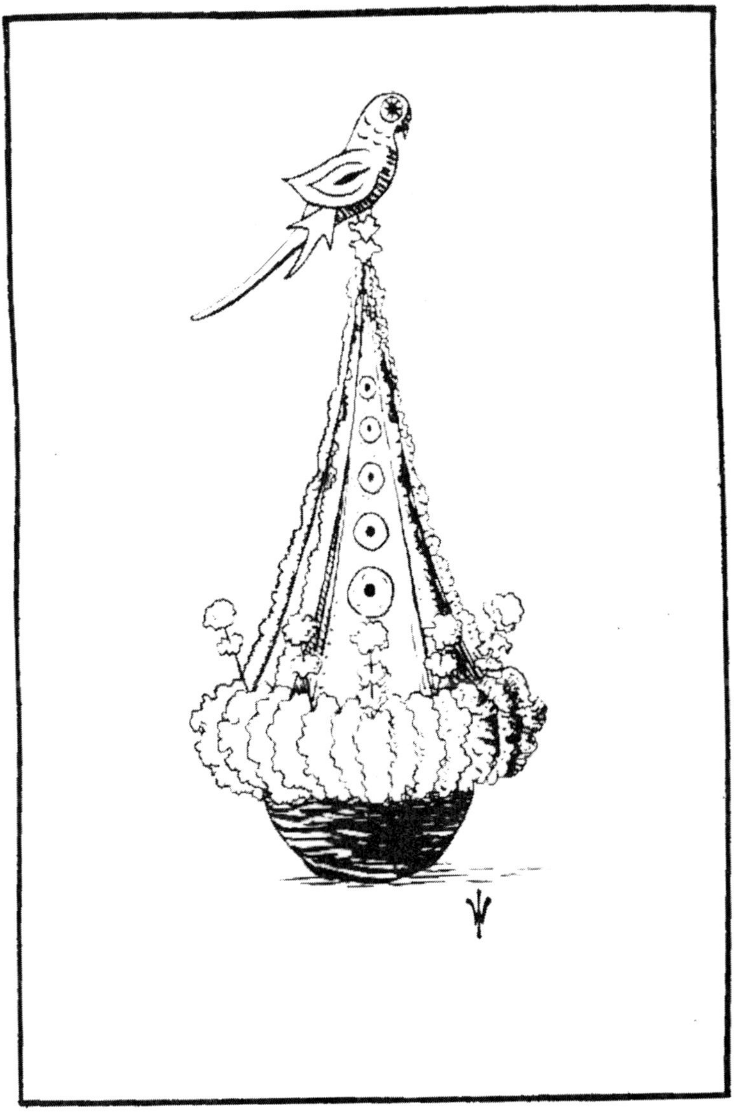

KARAGAM

PLATE IV

PŪJĀRĪ WITH ĀRATĪ

STONE SYMBOL OF POTU-RĀZU WITH STAKE FOR IMPALING ANIMALS

carried beyond the village limits. The villagers of the adjacent villages in their turn carry the karagam to the border of the next village, and in this way the karagam traverses many miles of country, and the baleful influence of the goddess is transferred to a safe distance."[1]

At another village I found that Kālīamma was represented by seven brass pots, without any water in them, one above the other, with margosa leaves stuck into the mouth of the topmost pot, as well as by an earthenware pot filled with water and also adorned with margosa leaves. It is possible that the seven brass pots represent seven sisters, or the seven virgins sometimes found in Tamil shrines. The people themselves have no idea what they mean, but can only say that it is Mamul, *i.e.* custom.

At Mysore City, in the Canarese country, I found, as stated above,[2] that the goddess was represented by a small metal pot full of water with a small mirror leaning against it. In the mouth of the pot two, four, or six *betel*[3] leaves are placed, always an even number, and the pot is decorated with a bunch of cocoanut flowers. The pot is called Kunna-Kannadi, eye-mirror, or Kalsa, and is used, I was told, as a symbol of deity in the preliminary ceremonies of all the Brāhmans. It is evidently connected with sun-worship, which in Mysore seems to have strongly influenced the cult of the village deities.

Another curious symbol much used in Mysore is called *ārati*.[4] It consists of a lamp made of rice flour about six or eight inches high, with the image of a face

[1] *Quarterly Journal of the Mythic Society*, Jan., 1920, p. 108.

[2] P. 29.

[3] Betel is a pepper plant, the leaf of which is wrapped round the nut of the areca palm and eaten by Indians as a digestive.

[4] The waving of a lamp in front of an image of a god is an orthodox Hindu custom. It is also frequently observed in the case of kings and other great personages. The object is to ward off the evil eye and other harmful influences. It is performed only by married women or nautch-girls. The name of the lamp and of the act of waving is *ārati*. See Dubois, *Hindu Manners and Customs*, p. 148. Hence the symbol described in the text.

roughly represented on one side of it by pieces of silver and blotches of kunkuma,[1] red paste, stuck on to represent the eyes, nose, mouth, etc. Sticks of incense were stuck in the lamp all round, and on the top were about four betel leaves stuck upright and forming a sort of cup with a wreath of white flowers below them. An āratī was brought to me at Mysore by the pūjārīs for my inspection. It was a quaint object, and seemed like the relic of some harvest festival of bygone days.

A common symbol of the village deities is simply a stick or a spear. It is very common in the Tamil country to see one or more iron spears stuck in the ground under a tree, to represent some village deity. The idea seems to be that the deity is represented by his weapons. In the Telugu country Potu-Razu, the brother or husband of the village goddess, is sometimes represented by a stone, sometimes by a thin wooden stake, like an attenuated post, about four or five feet high and roughly carved at the top. It faintly resembles a spear, and is called *śūlam*, which in Telugu means a spear.[2] Sometimes this stake stands beside a slab of stone representing Potu-Razu. At one village the symbol of Potu-Razu is a painted image made of wood, about three feet high, representing a warrior, sitting down with a sword in his hand, and carrying a lime and nine glass bangles belonging to his sister Ellamma. Beside each foot is the figure of a cock, and in the shrine is kept a large painted mask for the pūjārī to wear at festivals, as he dances round the image of Potu-Razu. But elaborate images of Potu-Razu of this kind are not very often found.

Another symbol akin to these stakes and spears is the Nattan Kal in the Tamil country. Nattan means "planted" and Kal means "a stone" or "post." The Nattan Kal is the first post of a nuptial booth, set up at an auspicious moment, painted red and white, adorned

[1] See p. 50.

[2] Siva's spear is called *śūal* in Sanskrit, and his trident is *triśūla*, three-spike.

with various decorations, and worshipped with offerings of cocoanuts and flowers. The symbolism is obscure.

The name is also applied to a small stone set up at the entrance to a village, which, according to a writer in the *Indian Interpreter*, who reviewed the first edition of this book in the January number, 1917, "is said to represent all the other Nads which are comprised in the particular district to which that place belongs," and is worshipped on the occasion of a marriage. The reviewer thinks that "it is evident that it points back to a time when people were not so numerous or so widely separated, and when all could come to the marriage festivities," and that "when that time passed some means had to be found for the representation of the others"; for this purpose a stone was erected to symbolize the clan and worship offered to it. It is probable, however, that the stone placed at the entrance of Tamil villages is akin to the *Boddu-rayee*, or navel-stone, set up at the foundation of a village in the Telugu country, as described below on page 60, which probably represents, like the boundary-stone, the spirit of the land on which the village is built.

The Nattan Kal set up for the wedding-booth may, in the same way, represent the spirit who presides over the procreation of children, and may possibly be a phallic emblem, like the lingam of Śiva.

Why stones or posts should in this way represent spirits it is difficult to explain. I have given below on page 148 what seems to me a possible explanation. But it must be admitted that all explanations can only be regarded as more or less probable hypotheses.

The shrines and images of Kogillu, a village in the Mysore country not far from Bangalore, are typical of that part of the country. At the extreme entrance to the village, near a tank, stands a small shrine of stone and mud sacred to the goddess Pūjāmma (she who is worshipped). On the stone door-posts are carved figures of serpents. Within the shrine there is no image of any kind, but on the left-hand side of the door is a platform, covered with garlands of white flowers, with a small earthenware lamp upon it, which is kept burning day and night as a symbol of the goddess.

To the right of this shrine stands a smaller one dedicated to a goddess called Dalamma. No one in the village could tell me who the goddess was nor what her name meant. There was no image nor lamp nor symbol of any kind in her shrine. An old picture frame, hung up on the wall to the left, without any picture in it, was the only attempt at decoration or symbolism. Just within the doorway was a shallow trough about one and a half feet long, one foot broad, and two inches deep, where the worshippers break their cocoanuts.

In front of the larger shrine stood an enclosure about five or six yards square, enclosed by a stone wall, with four slabs of stone in the centre, on which a platform is erected, covered by a canopy of cloth and leaves, during the annual festival. The lighted lamp is then brought out from the shrine, placed under the canopy, and worshipped as the symbol of the goddess. Apparently cattle are tethered in the enclosure at other times, and, when I saw it, there were no obvious marks of sanctity about it. About twenty yards off stands the Cattle Stone, a slab of rough stone about five feet high and three feet broad, set upon a stone platform about one and a half feet high. When the cattle get sore feet, their owners pour curds over the Cattle Stone for their recovery.

Near the Cattle Stone, in a field on the outskirts of the houses, stands a square stone pillar, about five feet high and half a foot in thickness, without any carving or ornament on it whatever. It represents Maramma, the goddess of small-pox and other epidemics, a most malignant spirit. Apparently she had been brought to this village by some people who had migrated from another village called Hethana; whence she is called Maramma-Hethana. Buffaloes and sheep are offered to her whenever epidemics break out.

The grāma-devatā herself—she has no other name—has in this village no permanent image. The goldsmith makes an image of clay in the form of a woman, about one or one and a half feet high, every year at the annual festival, which takes place after harvest, and she is then placed in the centre of the village under a canopy of green boughs. One striking feature of this festival is that on the first day of the festival a woman comes from every household to the place of worship with a lighted lamp made of rice flour, called ārati; and they all together wave their lamps in a circle from left to right above their heads and from right to left below.[1] When the festival is over, the washerman of the village, who acts as pūjārī, accompanied by all the villagers, takes the image to the tank, walks into the water, and leaves it there. In some villages in the Mysore State the ārati is presented by the men, the heads of the households, and not by the women. But in all the annual festivals in these parts the presentation of the ārati, which seems often to be regarded as a symbol of the deity herself, forms an important part of the ceremonial.

Ministrants. One of the most striking features of the worship of the village deities is the absence of anything like a sacerdotal caste in connexion with it. Every other department of village work belongs to a special caste, and in the ordinary worship of Vishṇu and Śiva the priestly caste of the Brāhmans is supreme. But in the worship of the village deities the pūjārīs are drawn from all the lower castes indiscriminately, though in any one village the pūjārīs of a particular goddess nearly always belong to one particular caste.

I have occasionally found a Brāhman in charge of a grāma-devatā shrine in the Tamil country. But then, as I have noted above, the Brāhman pūjārī never takes any part in the animal sacrifices, and, even so, is degraded by his connexion with the shrine. In the Telugu country the potters and the washermen, who are Śūdras of low caste, often officiate as priests, and

[1] See p. 39, n. 4.

an important part, especially in the buffalo sacrifices, is taken by the Mālās and Mādigās.[1]

A *Mādiga* nearly always kills the buffalo and performs the unpleasant ceremonies connected with the sprinkling of the blood, and there are certain families among the *Malās*, called *Asādis*, who are the nearest approach to a priestly caste in connexion with the village deities. They have the hereditary right to assist at the sacrifices, to chant the praises of the goddess while the sacrifices are being offered, and to perform certain ceremonies. But in the more primitive villages, where, it may be presumed, primitive customs prevail, it is remarkable how great a variety of people take an official part in the worship: the potter, the carpenter, the toddy-drawer, the washerman, Mālās and Mādigās, and even the Brāhman *Karṇam* or village accountant, have all their parts to play.

In the Tamil country this is not so marked, and the details of the worship are left far more to the regular pūjārī. It is noticeable that the office of pūjārī is by no means an honourable one, and this is especially the case among the Tamils, where Brāhman influence is strong and the shedding of blood is regarded with aversion. And even among the Brāhmans themselves, though they owe their influence to the fact that they are the priestly caste, the men who serve the temples are regarded as having a lower position in the caste than those Brāhmans engaged in secular pursuits.

Among the Canarese in the Bellary district the Asādis take a similar part in the worship to the Asādis in the Telugu country. In the whole of the Bellary district there are about sixty families of them living in three separate villages. They form practically a separate caste or section of the Outcastes. They eat food given them by the Mādigās and take their girls in marriage. The Asādi girls, however, never marry, but

[1] The Mālās and Mādigās are the chief groups of Outcastes in the Telugu country.

PLATE V

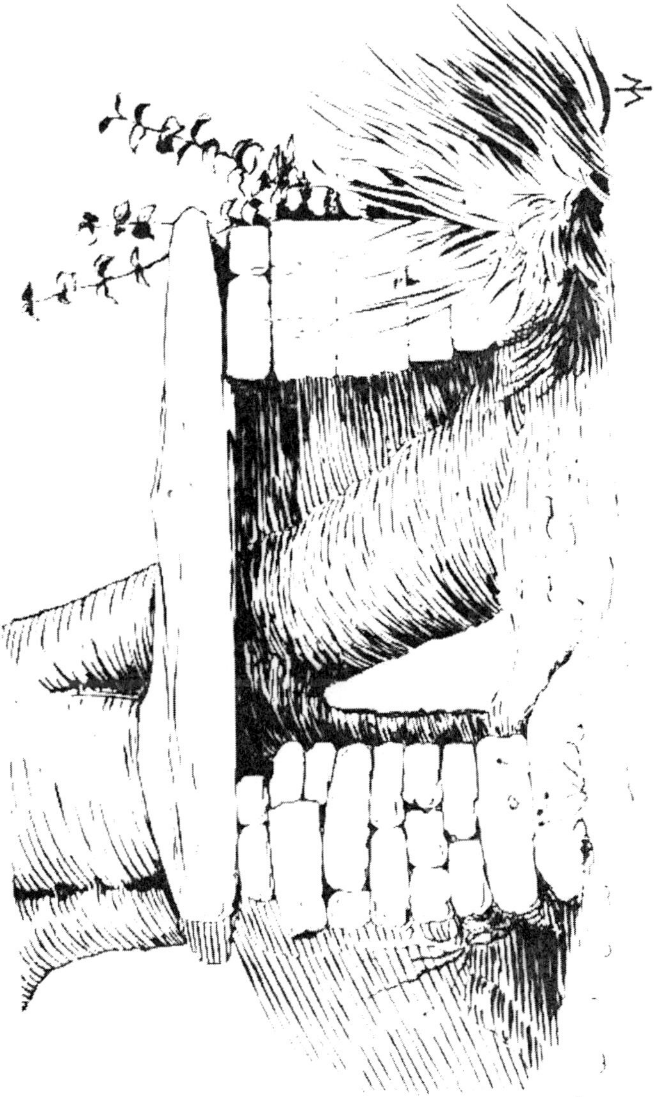

RUDE SHRINE AT FOOT OF TREE WITH BARE STONE AS SYMBOL

PLATE VI

RUDE SHRINE

MĪNĀCHĪ AND THE SEVEN SISTERS, CUDDALORE

are made *Basavīs*,[1] *i.e.* are consecrated to the goddess, and become prostitutes. Certainly the degradation of religion in India is seen only too plainly in the degradation of the priesthood.

Festivals. There is no act of uniformity and no ecclesiastical calendar regulating the festivals or forms of worship of village deities, and no universal custom as to the appointment of ministrants. In some villages, where there is a permanent shrine, offerings of rice, fruit, and flowers, with incense and camphor, are made every day by the villagers, who have made vows to the goddess, through the pūjārī. Often offerings are made once or twice a week, on fixed days, consisting chiefly of grain, fruit, and flowers and occasionally of goats, sheep, and fowls. In many places there is a fixed annual festival, which sometimes takes place after harvest, when the people are at leisure and well off for food; but there is no regular rule as to the time, and the custom varies widely in different districts. In most places, however, there is no regular annual festival, but sacrifices are offered whenever an epidemic or any other calamity occurs which may make it expedient to propitiate the goddess. In some villages old men complained to me that, whereas formerly sacrifices were offered yearly, now, owing to the decay of religion, they are only offered once in four or five years. So, again, there is no uniformity as to the duration of a festival. Generally it lasts about a week, but in the Tamil country it is sometimes a very elaborate affair, lasting for a fortnight, three weeks, or even a whole month; so too in some parts of the Canarese country the Māri festival, which is held in February, lasts for about four weeks. But a long festival is an expensive luxury, which only a large town or a well-to-do village is able to afford. Speaking generally, the object of the festival is simply to propitiate the goddess

[1] See Dubois, *Hindu Manners and Customs*, p. 133; Farquhar, *Modern Religious Movements in India*, p. 408. The word *basavī* is a feminine formed directly from *basava*, a bull. For *basava*, see below, p. 125, n. 1.

and to avert epidemics and other calamities from the village, and to ward off the attacks of evil spirits.

Every village in South India is believed by the people to be surrounded by evil spirits, who are always on the watch to inflict diseases and misfortunes of all kinds on the unhappy villagers. They lurk everywhere, on the tops of palmyra trees, in caves and rocks, in ravines and chasms. They fly about in the air, like birds of prey, ready to pounce down upon any unprotected victim, and the Indian villagers pass through life in constant dread of these invisible enemies. So the poor people turn for protection to the guardian deities of their village, whose function it is to ward off these evil spirits and protect the village from epidemics of cholera, small-pox, or fever, from cattle disease, failure of crops, childlessness, fires, and all the manifold ills that flesh is heir to in an Indian village.

The sole object, then, of the worship of these village deities is to propitiate them and to avert their wrath. There is no idea of praise and thanksgiving, no expression of gratitude or love, no desire for any spiritual or moral blessings. The one object is to get rid of cholera, small-pox, cattle disease, or drought, or to avert some of the minor evils of life. The worship, therefore, in most of the villages, only takes place occasionally. Sometimes, as I have stated above, there are daily offerings made to the deity; but, as a rule, the worship is confined to one big sacrifice, which takes place once a year, or on the occasion of some special disaster or outbreak of disease. The general attitude of the villager towards his village deity is "Let sleeping dogs lie." So long as everything goes on well and there is no disease afflicting man or beast, and no drought nor other great calamity, it seems safest to let her alone. But, when misfortune comes, it is a sign that she is out of temper, and it is time to take steps to appease her wrath.

I have dignified the periodical sacrifices to the village goddesses by the name of festivals. But the term is a misnomer. There is really nothing of a festal character about them. They are only gloomy and weird rites for the propitiation of angry deities or the driving away of evil spirits, and it is very difficult to detect any traces of a spirit of thankfulness or praise. Even the term worship is hardly correct. The object of all the various rites and ceremonies is not to worship the deity in any true sense of the word, but simply to propitiate it and avert its wrath. A brief description of the sacrifices and offerings themselves will make this clear. But I must premise that, as with the names and images and shrines, so with the offerings and sacrifices, there is no law of uniformity: the variations of local use and custom are innumerable. Still, the accounts here given will give a fair idea of the general type of rites and ceremonies prevalent throughout South India, in the propitation of village deities.

CHAPTER IV

MODES OF WORSHIP IN THE TELUGU COUNTRY

LET us suppose that an attack of cholera or small-pox has broken out in a village of South India. We will take a village in the Telugu country, in one of the more backward districts, where life is lived under more primitive conditions than in places where large towns and railways and the influence of the Brāhmans have tended to change old-fashioned ideas and customs.

A Telugu Village. The village deity, in this particular village, is called Peddamma, the great mother. The epidemic is a sign that she is angry and requires to be propitiated. So a collection is made for the expenses of a festival, or a rich man offers to pay all expenses, and a propitious day is selected, which in this village may be any day except Sunday or Thursday. Then the potter of the village is instructed to make a clay image of the great mother, and the carpenter to make a small wooden cart, and a buffalo is chosen as the chief victim for the sacrifice.

When the appointed day arrives, the buffalo is sprinkled all over with yellow *turmeric*,[1] while garlands of margosa leaves are hung round its neck and tied to its horns. At about two p.m. it is conducted round the village in procession to the sound of music and the beating of tom-toms. The two sections of the Outcastes, the Mālās and the Mādigās, take the leading

[1] *Curcuma longa* is an Indian plant from the rootstock of which a powder called turmeric is extracted. This powder is used as a dye and also as one of the ingredients of curry-powder.

part in the sacrifice, and conduct the buffalo from house to house. One Mādigā goes on ahead, with a tom-tom, to announce that "the buffalo devoted to the goddess is coming." The people then come out from their houses, bow down to worship the buffalo, and pour water over his feet, and also give some food to the Mālās and Mādigās, who form the procession. By about eight p.m. this ceremony is finished, and the buffalo is brought to an open spot in the village and tied up near a small canopy of cloths supported on bamboo poles, which has been set up for the reception of the goddess. All the villagers then assemble at the same place, and at about ten p.m. they go in procession, with music and tom-toms and torches, to the house of the potter, where the clay image is ready prepared. On arriving at his house, they pour about two and a half measures of rice on the ground and put the image on the top of it, adorned with a new cloth and jewels. All who are present then worship the image, and a ram is killed, its head being cut off with a large chopper, and the blood sprinkled on the top of the image, as a kind of consecration. The potter then takes up the idol and carries it out of the house for a little distance, and gives it to a washerman. who carries it to the place where the canopy has been set up to receive it. During the procession the people flourish sticks and swords and spears to keep off the evil spirits, and, for the same purpose, cut limes in half and throw them up in the air. The idea is that the greedy demons will clutch at the golden limes and carry them off, and so be diverted from any attack on the man who carries the image. When the idol has been duly deposited under the canopy, another procession is made to the house of the toddy-drawer. He is the man who climbs the palm trees and draws off the juice which is made into toddy. At his house some rice is cooked, and a pot of toddy and a bottle of *arrack*[1] are produced and duly smeared with yellow turmeric and a red paste, constantly used in religious

[1] Arrack is a native intoxicant.

worship among the Hindus and called *kunkuma*.[1] The cooked rice is put in front of the pot of toddy and bottle of arrack, a ram is killed in sacrifice, and then the toddy-drawer worships the pot and the bottle. The village officials pay him his fee, three-eighths of a measure of rice, three-eighths of a measure of *cholam*[2] and four annas, and then he carries the pot and bottle in procession, and places them under the canopy near the image of Peddamma. Then comes yet another procession. The people go off to the house of the chief official, the Reddy, and bring from it some cooked rice in a large earthenware pot, some sweet cakes, and a lamb. A large quantity of margosa leaves are spread on the ground in front of the image, the rice from the Reddy's house is placed upon them in a heap, and a large heap of rice, from one hundred to three hundred measures, according to the amount of the subscriptions, is poured in a heap a little farther away.

All these elaborate proceedings form only the preparations for the great sacrifice, which is now about to begin. The lamb is first worshipped and then sacrificed by having its throat cut and its head cut off. A ram is next brought and stood over the first large heap of rice, and is there cut in two, through the back, with a heavy chopper, by one of the village washermen. The blood pours out over the rice and soaks it through. One half of the ram is then taken up and carried to a spot a few yards off, where a body of Asādis are standing ready to begin their part in the ceremonies. The other half of the ram is left lying on the rice. The Asādis then begin to sing a long chant in honour of the deity. Meanwhile, the chief sacrifice is made. The buffalo is brought forward, and the Mādigās kill it by cutting its throat (in some villages its head is cut off). Some water is first poured over the blood, and then the pool of blood and water is covered up carefully with earth, lest any outsider from another

[1] Made of turmeric mixed with lime.
[2] A coarse grain, the staple food of the villagers.

PLATE VII

BUFFALO SACRIFICE

PLATE VIII

HEAD OF SACRIFICIAL BUFFALO

village should come and steal it. The idea is that if any man from another village should take away and carry home even a small part of the blood, that village would get the benefit of the sacrifice. The head of the buffalo is then cut off and placed before the image, with a layer of fat from its entrails smeared over the forehead and face, so as to cover entirely the eyes and nose. The right foreleg is cut off and placed crosswise in the mouth, some boiled rice is placed upon the fat on the forehead, and on it an earthenware lamp, which is kept alight during the whole of the festival. Why the right foreleg should be cut off and placed in the mouth, and what the meaning of it is, I have never been able to discover nor can I conjecture. When I have asked the villagers, they only reply, "It is the custom." But I have found the custom prevailing in all parts of South India, among Tamils, Telugus, and Canarese alike, and I have been informed that exactly the same custom prevails in the Southern Marāṭhā country. It seems to be a very ancient part of the ritual of sacrifice prevailing in South India.[1] This completes the presentation of the sacrifice to the goddess, who is supposed to delight in the food offered, and especially in the blood. A great deal of the food offered is, as a matter of fact, taken

[1] Maharaja Sir V. S. Raṅga Rao Bahadur, G.C.I.E., C.B.E., writes in *The Asiatic Review* for January, 1919: "The Lord Bishop wishes to know why the leg of an animal is put crosswise in its mouth after it has been sacrificed before the village goddess. Among the menial castes of a village there is the practice of a guilty man putting a piece of dry grass crosswise in his mouth when he goes to the head of his village to ask his pardon. It denotes that he has committed a wrong act, as a beast. In places where grass is not available, the person in question puts the first finger of his right hand crosswise in his mouth with the same idea or purpose. Here the animals are sacrificed before the village gods and goddesses by the people in the expectation, or rather with the firm belief, that their sins will be forgiven by those deities, and that their consequences will be thus averted by means of those sacrifices. Instead of putting their fingers in their mouths, as stated before, they put the animal's leg (generally the right leg) crosswise in its mouth. Though I am not sure that this is the explanation of this practice, I presume that it must be along these lines, as no other ground is traceable."

away by the people and eaten in their homes, but the idea is that the goddess takes the essence and leaves the worshippers the material substance. This takes till about three a.m. next morning; and then begins another important part of the ceremonies.

Some of the rice from the heap, over which the ram was sacrificed and its blood poured out, is taken and put in a flat basket, and some of the entrails of the buffalo are mixed with it. The intestines of the lamb, which was first killed, are put over the neck of a Mālā, and its liver is placed in his mouth,[1] while another Mālā takes the basket of rice soaked in blood and mixed with the entrails of the buffalo. A procession is then formed with these two weird figures in the middle. The man with the liver in his mouth is worked up into a state of frantic excitement and is supposed to be inspired by the goddess. He has to be held by men on either side of him, or kept fast with ropes, to prevent his rushing away; and all round him are the *ryots*, *i.e.* the small farmers, and the Mālās, flourishing clubs and swords, and throwing limes into the air, to drive away the evil spirits. As the procession moves through the village, the people shout out "Food! Food!" and the man who carries the basket sprinkles the rice soaked in blood over the houses to protect them from evil spirits. As he walks along, he shouts out, at intervals, that he sees the evil spirits, and falls down in a faint. Then lambs have to be sacrificed on the spot and limes thrown into the air and cocoanuts broken, to drive away the demons and bring the man to his senses. And so the procession moves through the village, amid frantic excitement, till, as the day dawns, they return to the canopy, where the great mother is peacefully reposing.

At about ten a.m. a fresh round of ceremonies begins. Some meat is cut from the carcass of the buffalo and cooked with some cholam, and then given to five little Mālā boys, *siddhalu*, the innocents, as they are called. They are all covered over with a large cloth,

[1] Cf. pp. 109, 148 below

and eat the food entirely concealed from view, probably to prevent the evil spirits from seeing them, or the evil eye from striking them. And then some more food is served to the Asādis, who have been for many hours, during the ceremonies of the night, chanting the praises of the goddess. After this the villagers bring their offerings. The Brāhmans, who may not kill animals, bring rice and cocoanuts, and other castes bring lambs, goats, sheep, fowls, and buffaloes, which are all killed by the washermen, by cutting their throats, except the buffaloes, which are always killed by the Mādigās, the lowest class of Outcastes. The heads are all cut off and presented to the goddess. This lasts till about three p.m., when the people go off to the house of the village carpenter, who has got ready a small wooden cart. On their arrival some cooked rice is offered to the cart, and a lamb sacrificed before it, and a new cloth and eight annas are given to the carpenter as his fee. The cart is then dragged by the washermen, to the sound of horns and tom-toms, to the place of sacrifice. The heads and carcasses of the animals already sacrificed are first removed by the Mālās and Mādigās, except the head of the buffalo first offered, which remains in its place till all the ceremonies are finished, when the shrine is removed.

At about seven p.m. another series of ceremonies begins. First a lamb is sacrificed before the goddess, and its blood mixed with some cooked rice, and at the same time a pig is buried up to the neck in a pit at the entrance of the village, with its head projecting above the earth. The villagers go in procession to the spot, while one of the Mādigās carries the rice, soaked in the blood of the lamb, in a basket. All the cattle of the village are then brought to the place and driven over the head of the unhappy pig,[1] which is, of course, trampled to death; and, as they pass over the pig, the blood and rice are sprinkled upon them to preserve them from disease. Then, after this, follows the final ceremony.

[1] Cf. p 58 below.

The image of the goddess is taken from the canopy by the washerman, and a Mādigā takes the head of the buffalo with its foreleg in the mouth, the forehead and nostrils all smeared over with fat, and the earthen lamp still lighted on the top. They then all go in procession to the boundary of the village, first the men carrying the buffalo's head, next the washerman with the image, and last the small wooden cart. When the procession arrives at the extreme limit of the village lands, they go on, for about a furlong, into the lands of the neighbouring village. There the Asādis first chant the praises of the goddess, then some turmeric is distributed to all the people, and finally the image is divested of all its ornaments and solemnly placed upon the ground and left there. The light on the head of the buffalo is extinguished, and the head itself carried off by the Mādigā, who takes it for a feast to his own house. The object of transporting the goddess to the lands of the next village is to transfer to that village the wrath of the deity, a precaution which does not show much faith in the temper of the goddess, nor much charity towards their neighbours!

Gudivada, near Masulipatam. A somewhat different form of ceremonial prevails in some of the villages of the Telugu country nearer the coast. The village of Gudivada, about twenty miles from the important town of Masulipatam, may be taken as a good specimen of a well-to-do village in a prosperous district, and the ceremonies prevailing there are a fair sample of the cult of the village deities in these parts.

The name of the village deity at Gudivada is Pallalamma. Her image is the figure of a woman with four arms, and a leopard's head under her right foot, carved in bas-relief on a flat stone about three feet high, standing in an open compound, surrounded by a low stone wall. The pūjārī, who is a Śūdra, gave me a full account of the rites and ceremonies. Weekly offerings are made every Sunday, when the pūjārī washes the image with water and soap-nut seeds early in the morning, and smears it with turmeric and kunkuma, offers incense, breaks a cocoanut, and cooks and presents to the image about a seer of rice, which he afterwards eats himself. The rice is provided daily by the villagers. Occasionally fowls and sheep are offered on the Sunday by villagers who have made vows in time of sickness or other misfortunes. When a sheep is sacrificed, it is first purified by washing. The animal is simply killed in front of the image by a Mādigā, who cuts off its head with a large chopper. The blood is allowed to flow on the ground and nothing special is done with it. The head becomes the perquisite of the pūjārī, and the offerer takes away the carcass for a feast in his house. In many villages, both in the Telugu and Tamil districts, water is poured over the sheep's back to see whether it shivers. If it shivers, it is a sign that the goddess has accepted it.[1] Where the people are economical, they keep on pouring water till it does shiver, to avoid the expense of providing a second victim, but, where they are more scrupulous, if it does not shiver, it is taken as a sign that the goddess will not accept it and it is taken away.

A public festival is held whenever an epidemic breaks out. The headman of the village then gets a new earthenware pot, besmears it with turmeric and kunkuma and puts inside some clay bracelets, some necklaces, and ear-rings, three pieces of charcoal, three pieces of turmeric, three pieces of incense, a piece of dried cocoanut, a woman's cloth, and two annas' worth of coppers—a strange collection of miscellaneous charms and offerings. The pot is then hung up in a tree near the image, as a pledge that, if the epidemic disappears, the people will celebrate a festival.

When it does disappear, a thatched shed of palmyra leaves is built near the image, and a special image of clay, adorned with turmeric and kunkuma, is put inside, and beneath it an earthen pot filled with buttermilk and boiled rice. This pot is also smeared with turmeric and

[1] For this widespread superstition see Sir Alfred Lyall, *Asiatic Studies*, i, 19. Cf. pp. 63, 68, 69, 73, 99, below.

kunkuma, adorned with margosa leaves, covered with an earthenware saucer, and carried in procession through the village during the day, to the exhilarating sound of pipes, horns, and tom-toms, by the village potter, who takes the rice and buttermilk for his perquisite and renews it every morning of the festival at the public expense. The duration of the festival depends on the amount of the subscriptions, but it always lasts for an odd number of days, excluding all numbers with a seven in them, *e.g.* 7, 17, 27, etc. During the night the barbers of the village chant the praises of the goddess, and the Mādigās beat tom-toms near the image.

On the night before the day appointed for the offering of animal sacrifices by the villagers, a male buffalo, called Devara Potu, *i.e.* devoted to the deity, is sacrificed on behalf of the whole village. First, the buffalo is washed with water, smeared with yellow turmeric and red kunkuma, and then garlanded with flowers and the leaves of the sacred margosa tree. It is brought before the image; and a Mādigā cuts off its head, if possible at one blow, over a heap of boiled rice, which becomes soaked with the blood. The right foreleg is then cut off and placed crosswise in its mouth, according to the widespread custom prevailing in South India, the fat of the entrails is smeared over the eyes and forehead, and the head is placed in front of the image. A lighted lamp is placed, not as in the other villages on the head itself, but on the heap of rice soaked with blood. This rice is then put into a basket; and a Mādigā, the village *vetty* or sweeper, carries it round the site of the village, sprinkling it on the ground as he goes. The whole village goes with him, but there is no music or tom-toms. The people shout out as they go "Poli! Poli!" *i.e.* "Food! Food!" and clap their hands and wave their sticks above their heads to keep off the evil spirits. The rice offered to the goddess, but not soaked with blood, is then distributed to the people. What spirits the rice soaked in blood is supposed to feed is not clear, but the object of sprinkling the blood is evidently to ward off evil spirits and prevent them from coming near the village, and apparently the present idea is that they will be satiated with rice and blood and not want to do any mischief. The original idea was possibly quite different; but this seems to be the intention of the ceremony in modern times.

On the next day, early in the morning, the clay image and the pot are washed and smeared afresh with turmeric and kunkuma. Incense and boiled rice are then offered as on other days, and the pot is taken in procession round the village. When this has been done, about midday, each householder brings his offering of boiled rice, cakes, fruits and flowers, and, in addition, the village as a whole contributes about two hundred or more seers of rice, which is boiled near the pandal. All these offerings are placed in a heap before the image. Then, first, a sheep or a buffalo is offered on behalf of the whole village. Having been duly washed, and smeared with turmeric and kunkuma, and decorated with margosa leaves, its head is cut off by a Mādigā. The blood is allowed to flow on the ground, and some loose earth is thrown upon it to cover it up. The head is offered to the image by the headman of the village. After this various householders, even Brāhmans and Bunniahs, bring animals for sacrifice. All are killed by a Mādigā, and then the heads are all presented and placed in a heap before the goddess. Sometimes an extraordinary number of animals is sacrificed on occasions of this kind, as many as a thousand sheep on a single day. In a village like Gudivada the number of victims is, of course, far less. The question of precedence in the offering of victims constantly gives rise to quarrels among the leading villagers. When I was once visiting Gudivada, there was a case pending before the *tahsildar*, *i.e.* the sub-divisional magistrate, between a *zamindar*, landowner, and a village *munsiff*, *i.e.* a village magistrate, about this knotty point. The heads are taken away by the pūjārīs, potters, washermen, barbers, Mālās and Mādigās, and others who take any official part in the sacrifice. The carcasses of the private sacrifices are taken away by the offerers, and that of the public victim belongs to the headman of the village. The rice, fruit, etc., are distributed among the various officials. The function lasts from about ten a.m. to five p.m.

In the evening, a cart is brought to the image with nine pointed stakes standing upright in it, two at each of the four corners and one in the centre: on each stake a young pig, a lamb, or a fowl is impaled alive. A Mālā, called a *Pambala, i.e.* hereditary priest, then sits in the cart dressed in female attire, holding in his hand the clay image of the goddess which was made for the festival. The cart is dragged with ropes to the extreme boundary of the village lands, and both cart and ropes are left beyond the boundary. The Pambalas take away the animals, which all die during the procession, as their share of the offerings.

Living animals impaled in many villages. This cruel ceremony of impaling live animals is quite common in the eastern part of the Telugu country,[1] and I have come across it in many villages that I have visited. The Rev. F. N. Alexander, the veteran C.M.S. missionary, who lived over fifty years at Ellore, told me that he witnessed it in the town of Ellore the first year that he went there, and wrote a letter to the *Madras Mail* describing it. As a result of his letter, the practice was forbidden by the Government. So now at Ellore the animals are tied on to the stakes without being impaled; but in many villages near Ellore the custom still survives of impaling the unfortunate animals alive. Sometimes there are only four stakes on the cart, sometimes five, and sometimes more. It is not often that there are as many as nine. In one of the villages of the Kurnool district, I found that a similar barbarity was practised in connexion with the hook-swinging ceremony. On the fifth day of the festival in honour of Aṅkalamma, a large car is constructed, with an arrangement of poles projecting

[1] Cf. pp. 59, 65, 69.

about 20 feet in the air. A sheep is then suspended from the pole by iron hooks fastened through the muscles of its back and a band round its middle, and swung round and round. Two or three of the older men in the village said that they had often seen men swing like this with iron hooks fastened into their backs,[1] and that it did not hurt. As soon as the sheep is swung up, buffaloes, sheep and goats are sacrificed, and the car is then dragged in procession through the village.

A cruel pig sacrifice. Sometimes, when there is cattle disease, a pig is buried up to its neck at the boundary of the village, a heap of boiled rice is deposited near the spot, and then all the cattle of the village are driven over the unhappy pig.[2] It is not the custom at Gudivada to sprinkle anything on the cattle as they pass over the poor animal, as is done elsewhere.

There is a remarkable parallel to this form of sacrifice in a description quoted by Mr. E. Thurston, in his *Ethnographical Notes in Southern India*,[3] of an ancient custom among the Lambadis, a wandering tribe of South India:

> "In former times, the Lambadis, before setting out on a journey, used to procure a little child and bury it in the ground up to its shoulders, and then drive their loaded bullocks over the unfortunate victim. In proportion to the bullocks thoroughly trampling the child to death, so their belief in a successful journey increased."

It is possible that this custom of driving the cattle over the head of a buried pig may be connected with the worship of an agricultural goddess, since in ancient Greece the pig was sacred to agricultural deities, *e.g.* Aphrodite, Adonis, and Demeter; but it may also be a survival of some former custom of infanticide or human sacrifice such as prevailed among the Lambadis.

An old man in the Kurnool district once described to me the account that he had received from his fore-

[1] This is the practice in the Hindu *dola-jātra*, swing-festival, celebrated in honour of Durgā, the wife of Śiva. Cf. pp. 61, 76, 82, 83.

[2] See p. 53, 60.

[3] P. 507.

fathers of the ceremonies observed when founding a new village. An auspicious site is selected and an auspicious day, and then in the centre of the site is dug a large hole, in which are placed different kinds of grain, small pieces of the five metals, gold, silver, copper, iron, and lead, and a large stone, called *boddu-rayee*, *i.e.* navel-stone, standing about three and a half feet above the ground, very like the ordinary boundary stones seen in the fields. And then, at the entrance of the village, in the centre of the main street, where most of the cattle pass in and out on their way to and from the fields, they dig another hole and bury a pig alive. This ceremony would be quite consistent with either of the explanations suggested as to the origin of pig-burying. The pig may be buried at the entrance to the village as the emblem of fertility and strength, to secure the prosperity of the agricultural community, the fertility of the fields, and the health and fecundity of the cattle. Or it may equally be a substitute for an original human sacrifice. The idea that a new building or institution must be inaugurated by the sacrifice of a human life is very common all over India. To this day there is often a panic among the villagers who live near the banks of a river where a bridge is about to be built, because they think that one or more of their babies are sure to be required to bury under the foundations of the first pier. On one of my visits to Kalasapad, in the Cuddapah district, the missionary told me that, when a new ward was opened for their local mission dispensary, no one would go into it, because the people imagined that the first to go in would be the needful sacrifice. Their fears were allayed by a religious service at the opening of the ward; but had it been a Hindu hospital, probably a goat or a sheep would have been killed as a substitute for the human victim.

The idea of substitution, too, is quite common in India. In the hook-swinging ceremony described above,[1]

[1] P. 59.

it is common both in the Telugu and Tamil districts to substitute a sheep for a man, and to fasten the iron hooks in the muscles of its back.

Alleged infanticide among Todas. I have been told that, among the Todas of the Nilgiri Hills, it was formerly the custom to place female children, whom it was not desired to rear, on the ground at the entrance of the mund, *i.e.* a group of huts, and drive buffaloes over them. If they survived this ordeal, they were allowed to live.

It is only fair to add that the Todas themselves deny that this custom ever existed. To quote Mr. Thurston again:[1]

"The practice of infanticide, as it prevailed among the Todas of the Nilgiris, is best summed up in the words of an aged Toda during an interview with Colonel Marshall (*A Phrenologist amongst the Todas*, 1873): 'I was a little boy when Mr. Sullivan (the first English pioneer of the Nilgiris) visited these mountains. In those days it was the custom to kill children, but the practice has long died out, and now one never hears of it. I don't know whether it was wrong or not to kill them, but we were very poor, and could not support our children. Now every one has a mantle (*putkūli*), but formerly there was only one for the whole family. We did not kill them to please any god, but because it was our custom. The mother never nursed the child, and the parents did not kill it. Do you think we could kill it ourselves? Those tell lies who say we laid it before the open buffalo-pen so that it might be run over and killed by the animals. We never did such things, and it is all nonsense that we drowned it in buffalo's milk. Boys were never killed—only girls; not those who were sickly and deformed—that would be a sin; but, when we had one girl, or in some families two girls, those that followed were killed. An old woman (kelachi) used to take the child immediately it was born, and close its nostrils, ears and mouth with a cloth thus (here pantomimic action). It would shortly droop its head, and go to sleep. We then buried it in the ground. The kelachi got a present of four annas (4d.) for the deed.' The old man's remark about the cattle-pen refers to the Malagasy custom of placing a new-born child at the entrance of a cattle-pen, and then driving the cattle over it, to see whether they would trample on it or not."

Masulipatam. At Masulipatam, where ceremonies are performed very similar to those at Gudivada

[1] *Op. cit.*, p. 507.

during an epidemic, a washerman carries the earthenware pot, half full of buttermilk and adorned with margosa leaves, round the village to the sound of tom-toms. As it goes round, the washerman stops at each house and the wife comes out and pours water beside the pot on the ground and does reverence to the pot, imploring the goddess not to let any evil spirit come to the house; and then she puts more rice and buttermilk into it. When it is full, it is taken back to the shrine and another brought in its place. As this procession continues for fifteen days, the accumulation of rice and buttermilk must be considerable. It is ultimately consumed by the washermen, potters, Mālās and Mādigās, who take part in the festival. The real sacrifice begins on the sixteenth day and lasts for a month. Cotton-thread and all the rice and buttermilk collected from the villagers are offered to the image. The images themselves are smeared with turmeric, and dots of kunkuma are put on them, and finally on the last day a male buffalo, called *Devara-Potu*, *i.e.* devoted to the goddess, is brought before the image and its head cut off by the head Mādigā of the town. The blood is caught in a vessel and sprinkled over some boiled rice, and then the head, with the right foreleg in the mouth, is placed before the shrine on a flat wicker basket, with the rice and blood on another basket just below it. A lighted lamp is placed on the head, and then another Mādigā carries it on his own head round the village, with a new cloth dipped in the blood of the victim tied round his neck. This is regarded here and elsewhere as a very inauspicious and dangerous office; and the headman of the village has to offer considerable inducements to persuade a Mādigā to undertake it. Ropes are tied round his body and arms and held fast by men walking behind him, as he goes round, to prevent his being carried off by evil spirits, and limes are cut in half and thrown into the air, so that the demons may catch at them instead of at the man. It is believed that gigantic demons sit on the tops of tall trees ready to swoop down and carry him away, in order to get the rice and the buffalo's head. The idea of carrying the head and rice round a village, so the people said, is to draw a kind of cordon on every side of it and prevent the entrance of the evil spirits. Should any one in the town refuse to subscribe for the festival, his house is omitted from the procession, and left to the tender mercies of the devils. This procession is called *bali haranam*;[1] and in this district *inams*, rent-free lands, are held from Government by certain families of Mādigās for performing it. Besides the buffalo, large numbers of sheep and goats and fowls are sacrificed, each householder giving at least one animal. The head Mādigā who kills the animals takes the carcass and distributes the flesh among the members of his family. Often cases come into the courts to decide who has the right to kill them. As the sacrifice cannot wait for the tedious processes of the law, the elders of the village settle the question at once, pending an appeal to the courts. But in the town of Masulipatam, a Mādigā is specially licensed by the Municipality for the purpose, and all disputes are avoided.

Cocanada. At Cocanada there is only one Grāma-Devatā, Nukalamma (from Nuku, a Tamil word, meaning "to beat"); but she is very ill-tempered, they told me, and gives much trouble. Curiously enough, the present pūjārī is a woman of the fisherman caste. The office was hereditary in her family and she is the only surviving member of it. A male relative acts as deputy-pūjārī. Offerings are made to Nukalamma every day, doubtless on account of her temper. One custom I found observed here, which is not uncommon in these parts. When a victim's head has been cut off, it is put before the shrine and water poured on it. The offerer then waits to see whether the mouth opens. If it does, it is a sign that the sacrifice is accepted.[2] Another ceremony observed here is significant and, doubtless, a relic of the primitive idea

[1] Sanksrit for "presentation of the offering."
[2] See p. 55 n. 1, above.

of sacrifice. As soon as the victim is killed, the offerer dips his finger in the blood and puts it on his own forehead.

The annual festival of this goddess lasts for a whole month, ending on the New Year's day of the Telugu calendar. During this festival the procession of pots is observed with special ceremony. Six brass pots, each about two feet high, with the figure of a cobra springing from below the neck and rising over the mouth of the pot, are draped with women's cloths and carried round the town on men's head. Nothing is put inside them, but, as they go round, the women of each house come out, pour water on the feet of the bearers, and make offerings of rice and fruit. These are solemnly presented to the pots by the bearers, and some powder is applied to the two small feet that project at the base of each pot, and form a sort of frame fitting on the bearer's head. The bearer then takes a little of the turmeric powder, that is already on the foot of the pot, and puts it into the dish in which the offering was brought, with a few margosa leaves from a bundle that he carries with him. The dish is returned to the woman who offered the gifts, which become the property of the pūjārī. The women and children of the family mark their foreheads with the turmeric, and put the margosa leaves in their hair. This is called *Ammavari-Prasādam.*[1] As they go round, the pūjārīs dance to the sound of tom-toms.

On the last day of the festival, when a buffalo is sacrificed, a curious ceremony takes place which is said to be very common in the villages of this district. After the head is cut off by the vetty,[2] who is a Mādigā, the blood is collected in a basin and nine kinds of grain and *gram*[3] are put into it. The basin is then put before the idol inside the shrine, and the

[1] The turmeric and the margosa leaves are a gift of grace (Sanskrit *prasāda*, grace) from the goddess. Food and water from the table of a Hindu god given to the worshippers in the temple are called *prasāda*.

[2] See above p. 56.

[3] *Gram* is coarse lentils.

doors of the shrine are kept shut for three days. On the fourth day the doors are opened, the coagulated mass of blood, grain, and gram is carefully washed, and the grain and gram are separated on the ground behind the shrine, in order to see which of the various kinds of grain has sprouted. All the ryots eagerly assemble to watch the result, and whichever is found to have sprouted, is regarded as marked out by the goddess as the right kind of grain to sow that year. This method of determining which crop to sow is common in both the Godavari and Masulipatam districts. In these sacrifices to Nukalamma, too, the application of the blood is specially noticeable. As soon as the victim is killed, a small quantity of the blood is smeared on the sides of the door-posts of the shrine; the deputy-pūjārī dips his finger in the blood and applies it to his forehead; then all the other people present do the same; and afterwards some boiled rice and some turmeric powder are mixed with the blood, and a little of the mixture is sprinkled on the head of the Mādigā who holds the basin to catch the blood.

When an epidemic of cholera breaks out, another goddess, called Maridiamma, is installed in the place of the Nukalamma. A log of margosa wood, about three feet high and six inches in diameter, is cut and roughly carved at the top into the shape of a head, and then fixed in the ground with a pandal of leaves and cloths over it. Then the procession of the earthen pot half filled with buttermilk and rice is conducted, very much in the same way as at Masulipatam,[1] every day till the epidemic subsides. After that, some ten or twelve small carts are made, about six feet square, with three pointed stakes standing up on each side, on which live animals are impaled, as in other parts of the Telugu country.[2] The carts are partly filled with boiled rice and curry stuff prepared at the shrine, the blood of the victims sacrificed being poured over the rice. I was told that live animals were only impaled if a cart did

[1] See p. 62 above. [2] See p. 58 above.

not move properly as it was dragged to the boundary, since that is regarded as a sign that the goddess is angry and needs to be appeased.

Ellore. The number of victims slaughtered at some of these festivals is enormous. At Ellore, which is a town of considerable size and importance, I was told that at the annual festival of Mahālakshmī about a a thousand animals are killed in one day, rich people sending as many as twenty or thirty. The blood then flows down into the fields behind the place of sacrifice in a regular flood, and carts full of sand are brought to cover up what remains on the spot. The heads are piled up in a heap about fifteen feet high in front of the shrine, and a large earthen basin about one-and-a-half feet in diameter is then filled with gingelly oil and put on the top of the heap, a thick cotton wick being placed in the basin and lighted. The animals are all worshipped with the usual *namaskāram*, *i.e.* folded hands raised to the forehead, before they are killed. This slaughter of victims goes on all day.

At midnight about twenty or twenty-five buffaloes are sacrificed. Their heads are cut off by a Mādigā pūjārī and with their carcasses are thrown upon large heaps of rice which have been presented to the goddess, till the rice is soaked with blood.

The subsequent ceremonies illustrate again the varieties of local custom. The rice is collected in about ten or fifteen large baskets, and, instead of being carried by a Mādigā, is carried on a large cart drawn by buffaloes or bullocks, with the Mādigā pūjārī seated on it. As the cart moves along, Mādigās sprinkle the rice on the streets and on the walls of the houses shouting "Poli! Poli!" ("Food! Food!"). A large body of men of different castes, Śūdras, Kommas, and Outcastes, go with the procession: but only the Mādigās and Mālās (the two sections of the Outcastes) shout "Poli," the rest following in silence. They have only two or three torches to show them the way, and no tom-toms nor music. Apparently the idea is that, if they make a noise or display a blaze of light, they will attract the evil spirits, who will swoop down on them and do them some injury; though in other villages it is supposed that a great deal of noise and flourishing of sticks will keep the evil spirits at bay. Before this procession starts, the heads of the buffaloes are placed in front of the shrine, with the right foreleg in the mouth, the fat from the entrails smeared about half an inch thick over the whole face, and a large earthen lamp on the top of each head. The Pambalas[1] play tom-toms and chant a long story about Gaṅgamma till daybreak. About eight a.m. they put the buffalo heads with the lighted lamps upon them into separate baskets; and these are carried in procession through the town to the sound of tom-toms. All castes follow, shouting and singing. In former times, I was told, there was a good deal of fighting and disturbance during this procession, but now the police maintain order. When the procession arrives at the municipal limits, the heads are thrown over the boundary, and left there. The people then all bathe in the canal and return home.

On the last day of the festival, which, I may remark, lasts for about three months, a small cart is made of margosa wood and a stake is fixed at each of the four corners. A pig and a fowl are tied to each stake, while a fruit, called *dubakaya*, is impaled on it instead of the animal. A yellow cloth, sprinkled with the blood of the buffaloes, is tied round the sides of the cart, and some margosa leaves are tied round the cloth. A Pambala sits on the cart, to which are fastened two large ropes, each about 200 yards long. Then men of all castes, without distinction, lay hold of the ropes and drag the cart round the town to the sound of tom-toms and music. Finally it is brought outside the municipal limits and left there, the Outcastes taking away the animals and fruits.

Sometimes, I was told, animals are sacrificed to Gaṅgamma by the people in Ellore in the courtyards of their own houses. They then clean the wall of

[1] See p. 58 above.

the house outside with cow-dung and make three horizontal lines with kunkuma (a red paste of turmeric and lime), with a dot above and below, and a semicircle on the right side with a dot in the middle, thus:—

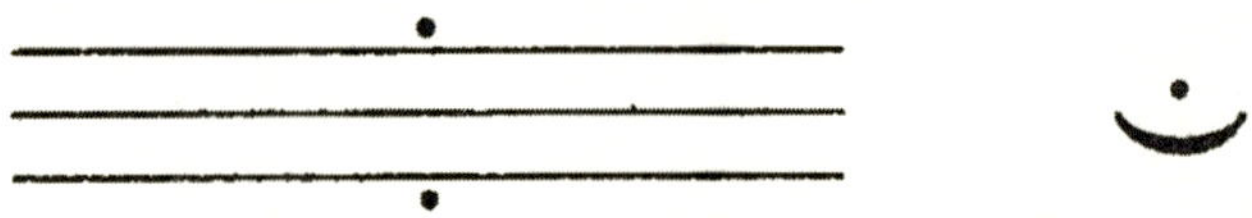

The symbol on the right represents the sun and moon: that on the left is the Śaivite sectarian mark. They sacrifice to these symbols sheep, goats, and fowls. It is curious that, in these private sacrifices at home, they pour water on the sheep and goats to see whether they shiver, as a sign of acceptance,[1] though this is not done in the public sacrifices at Ellore.

Dharmaja-Gudem, near Ellore. At a village called Dharmaja-Gudem, about sixteen miles from Ellore, while the main features of the festivals are the same as those found elsewhere, there are two or three peculiarities, which deserve notice. The ordinary grāma-devatās of the village are Ellaramma, Gaṅgamma, Mutyalamma, and Ravelamma, who are represented by four stone pillars about six feet high, with figures of women carved on them, standing in an open field on the outskirts of the village: but when an epidemic breaks out, Mutyalamma, Gaṅgamma, Aṅkamma and Mahālakshmīamma are the deities propitiated, and special images are made of them. Those of the first three are made of clay, but that of Mahālakshmīamma is made of turmeric kneaded into a paste. Then, again, it is noticeable that a Brāhman acts as pūjārī of Mahālakshmī, a washerman as pūjārī of Gaṅgamma, and a potter as pūjārī of Aṅkamma. The Brāhman pūjārī presides over the worship for the greater part of the festival, which lasts for about three months, and during that time the people come almost every day and offer flowers, fruits, cocoanuts, camphor and incense, but no animal sacrifices. All this time, too, some nautch-

[1] See p. 55 above.

girls come and dance in a booth erected in front of the image and work themselves up into a state of frenzy, during which they are supposed to be inspired by the deities, and utter oracles to the worshippers. When the epidemic begins to abate, the Brāhman pūjārī closes his part of the proceedings and departs.

Then, on that afternoon and evening, animal sacrifices are offered under the booth. On the first animal killed, which is generally a goat, water is poured from a brass vessel, to see if it shivers.[1] If it does, it is taken as a good omen that the goddess is propitiated and the disease will disappear. Then other animals are brought and, in accordance with a very common division of functions in the Telugu country, a washerman kills the sheep, goats, and fowls, and a Mādigā the buffaloes. The heads of the sheep and goats, as well as of the buffaloes, have the right forelegs put crosswise in the mouths, the faces smeared with fat from the entrails, and a lighted lamp placed above them. The blood is caught in a basket full of boiled rice, and the rice and blood are sprinkled round the village, while a Mādigā carries on his own head the head of a buffalo exactly as is done elsewhere. Here, too, great care is taken to prevent any person from another village taking away any of the rice and blood, lest the other village should get all the benefit of the sacrifice, and evils of all kinds descend on the unhappy villagers who have offered it. The ceremony of impaling live animals on stakes fixed round a wooden car,[2] and dragging them off to the boundary of the village is also practised here.

Bhīmadole, near Ellore. At another village, called Bhīmadole, about twenty miles from Ellore, I came across one of the few instances I have met with of any direct connexion between the harvest and the worship of a village goddess. There is an annual festival held there about harvest time, in November or December, lasting one day, which is always a Tuesday. About half a ton of rice is boiled in the middle of the village, taken

[1] See page 55. [2] See p. 58.

to the shrine and presented in a heap before the image, with a lighted lamp on the top of it, made of rice flour kneaded into a paste, and holding about one pint of oil.[1] Some toddy is poured on the ground to the east of the rice by the washerman ; incense and camphor are burnt ; while the people make namaskāram (salutation with folded hands raised to the forehead) to the image. As many as two hundred sheep and goats are then killed, and fowls are brought by the poorer people. In this festival, the rice soaked in the blood of the victims is not sprinkled on the streets of the village nor over the houses, but each ryot gives a handful of it to one of his field servants (an Outcaste), who takes and sprinkles it over his master's fields. Three handfuls of the crop are cut on the same day to inaugurate the harvest. No buffaloes are sacrificed during this festival.

On the other hand, when an epidemic breaks out, there is a special festival, in which five or six buffaloes are sacrificed as well as about three hundred sheep and goats. The buffaloes are killed last of all. One special buffalo, called *Pedda-Veta*, great sacrifice, is reserved to the end, and killed at about ten p.m. Nothing special is done with the blood of the other buffaloes nor with that of the sheep and goats, but the blood of the Pedda-Veta is allowed to flow on to some of the rice, as soon as the head is severed, and both head and carcass are placed upon the rice heap. The head, as usual, has the right foreleg put in the mouth, with fat smeared over the face and a lighted lamp above it.

At about eleven p.m. the head is carried by a Mālā, not by a Mādigā in this village, on his own head three times round the boundaries of the village site, and the rice soaked in blood is sprinkled by the Mālās on the ground, as they go, and on any cattle they happen to meet, accompanied by the same weird and excited procession as elsewhere.

The illustration facing this page represents a shrine of Poshamma, a goddess worshipped by the Mālās. On the top of the shrine stands an earthenware lamp.

[1] See p. 39.

PLATE IX

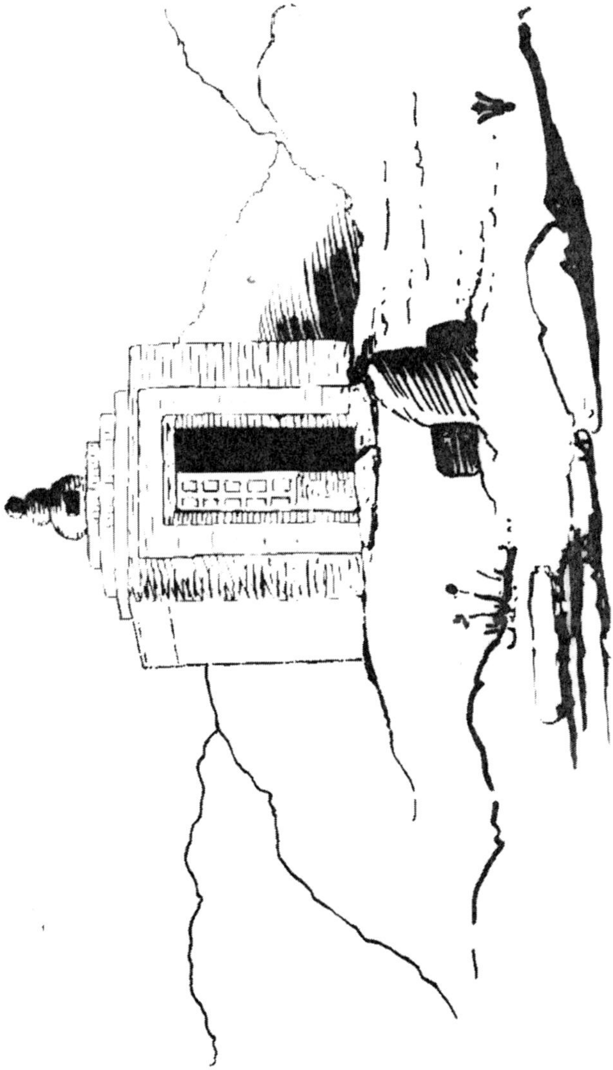

SHRINE OF POSHAMMA

PLATE X

KUTTANDEVAR

CHAPTER V

MODES OF WORSHIP IN THE CANARESE COUNTRY

THE Canarese are closely allied ethnologically to the Telugus, and we should naturally expect, therefore, to find a close connexion between the ceremonies used by the two peoples in the worship of their village goddesses. A brief account of the ceremonies used in different parts of the Canarese country will show how far this is actually the case.

Bellary District. In the Bellary district Durgamma,[1] Suṅkalamma, and Uramma are very commonly worshipped. Uramma means simply the village goddess, and is equivalent to the general term grāma-devatā. Her festival is not celebrated annually, but when there is a specially good crop, or when cholera or plague break out. The following account of it was given me by an Asādi of a village near Bellary, and may be taken as describing fairly the general type of such festivals and sacrifices throughout the district.

We will suppose that cholera has broken out in the village. The villagers then make vows to offer the sacrifice if the epidemic ceases. The day appointed for the festival is invariably a Tuesday, and on the previous Tuesday a basin-shaped earthen lamp, filled with oil and furnished with a stout cotton wick, is placed in the house of the *Reddy* (village magistrate) and kept lighted till the festival and all the ceremonies are ended. The carpenter, also, prepares beforehand a wooden image of the goddess and a small cart, while

[1] Durgā is one of the many names of Kālī, the wife of Śiva.

a *pandal* (booth) of leaves and cloths, with a raised platform inside and festoons of flowers hung in front, is made ready in an open space in the village. On the appointed Tuesday a sheep or goat is first sacrificed at the carpenter's house, and the carcass given to the *taliāris* (village servants, generally Boyas by caste).

The image is then put on the cart about sunset, and taken by the villagers in procession to the booth. In some villages the washerman lays clean cloths on the ground, so that the men who carry the image from the cart to the booth may not tread on the earth. Then the people proceed to the house of the flower-seller, who is by caste a Gira and generally a *Liṅgāyat*[1] by religion, and bring thence a kind of cradle, made of pith and flowers, together with a pot of toddy, a looking-glass, some limes, and other articles used in worship. The cradle and looking-glass are hung up in front of the booth, and the other things are placed in front of the image. A looking-glass, I was told, is considered very auspicious, and is used by all castes in various religious ceremonies. Next, the lighted lamp is brought in procession from the Reddy's house and placed before the image by some man belonging to the Reddy's family. Four measures of boiled rice are then poured in a heap before the image, while flowers, betel leaves, nuts, plantains, and cocoanuts are offered, and camphor and incense burnt.

When the preliminaries have been duly performed, the buffalo, which, from the close of the last festival, has been dedicated to the goddess and reserved for sacrifice, is brought from the Outcaste quarters to the pandal in solemn procession, the Asādis, some ten or twelve in number, dancing before it and singing songs in honour of the goddess. It has been kept the whole day without food or water and is garlanded with flowers and smeared with turmeric and red kunkuma. This

[1] A South Indian Śivaite sect, named Liṅgāyats, because each wears a small *Liṅga* (Śiva's phallic emblem) hung round his neck in a reliquary.

buffalo is called *Gauda-Kona* or husband-buffalo, and, according to the traditional story, represents the Outcaste husband who pretended to be a Brāhman and married the Brāhman girl, now worshipped as Uramma. A fresh buffalo is always dedicated immediately after the festival, lest the goddess should be left a widow. When it arrives at the pandal, it is laid on its side upon the ground and its head is cut off by one of the Mādigās with the sacrificial chopper. Its neck is placed over a small pit, which has been dug to receive the blood, and the entrails are taken out and placed in the pit with the blood. The right leg is then cut off below the knee and put cross-wise in the mouth, some fat from the entrails is placed on the forehead and a small earthenware lamp, about as large as a man's two hands, with a wick as thick as his thumb, is placed on the fat and kept there lighted, till the festival is over. Some of the blood and entrails are then mixed with some boiled rice and placed in a new basket, which a Mādigā, stripped naked, places on his head and takes round the boundary of the village fields, accompanied by a washerman carrying a torch, and followed by a few of the villagers. He sprinkles the rice, blood, and entrails all round the boundary. The greatest care is taken to see that none of the blood from the pit in front of the pandal, where the buffalo was killed, is taken away by any one from another village, as they believe that in that case all the benefits of the sacrifice would be transferred to the other village. In former days men who stealthily took away the blood were chased and murdered. As this cannot be done under British rule, a strict patrol is kept all round the place where the blood lies, and no one from any other village is allowed to loiter near the spot.

Next day, Wednesday, about four p.m., villagers, who have made vows, bring sheep for sacrifice and offerings of boiled rice, fruits, cocoanuts, etc., with incense and camphor. I was told that fowls were not offered to Uramma. After the sheep has been killed, the head is cut off and water is poured on the nose; if the mouth opens, it is regarded as a good omen. The carcasses are taken away by the offerers to their own homes as a feast for the family. The heads are all put together and distributed to those of the village artisans and officials who are meat-eaters.

On Thursday, about four p.m., the flesh of the buffalo, which was sacrificed on Tuesday evening and must be by this time rather high, is cooked in front of the pandal, and part of it is first offered to the goddess, with some boiled rice, on five separate leaves. The Asādis make the offering with songs and dances, the breaking of cocoanuts, and burning of incense and camphor, and prostrations on the ground, *shasthāngam.* For this part of their service they receive twenty pies (about 1⅔d.), four pies for each leaf, not an extravagant sum. Then they take the five leaves away and eat the flesh and rice at some distance from the pandal, where it was cooked. These offerings to the goddess must be eaten on the spot, and are not allowed to be taken home. The rest of the flesh is given to the Outcastes and taliāris, who cook and eat some of it on the spot and take away the remainder. After sunset the goddess is put on the wooden cart and dragged in procession to the boundary of the village, an Asādi walking in the front and carrying on his head the head of the buffalo. When they come to the limit of the village lands, they leave the image on their own side of the boundary and there it stays. This ceremony ends the festival.

Bellary Town. Somewhat similar festivals are held periodically to propitiate Suṅkalamma, the goddess of small-pox and measles, and Maramma, the goddess of cholera. In the town of Bellary there is a shrine of Durgamma[1] which consists only of an ant-hill, with a plain stone shrine about thirty feet long, six deep and eight or ten high built over it. The story goes that an old woman many years ago was worshipping an image of Durgamma on this spot, when the goddess appeared to her and said that she was Durgamma of Bellary, that

[1] See p. 71, n. 1, above.

she lived in the ant-hill, and ought to be worshipped there. The ant-hill grew in seize in the course of years and a shrine was built. The present pūjārī, who is a Golla or milkman by caste, says that in the time of his father, about forty years ago, a large snake lived in the ruined wall behind the shrine, and used to come out and eat eggs and milk placed for it before the shrine. Apparently it very rarely makes its appearance now.

There is an annual festival to this goddess in Bellary, when male buffaloes, sheep, goats, and fowls are offered in sacrifice. When a buffalo is sacrificed, the right leg is, as usual, cut off and placed in its mouth, and fat is smeared over its forehead, with a lighted lamp on the top. Then the offerer stands with folded hands in front of the goddess asking for a boon; and, if at that time the mouth of the buffalo opens, he thinks that his prayer has been granted; otherwise he goes away disappointed. The tahsildar of Bellary conjectured that the practice of putting the right foreleg in the mouth was originally connected with this last ceremony, its object being to prevent *rigor mortis* setting in at once, and to keep the mouth open and the jaws twitching, so as to deceive the superstitious. But this does not seem to be a likely explanation of so widespread a custom. The skins of the buffaloes offered in sacrifice are used for the drums employed in worship, and the carcasses are given to the Outcastes and taliāris in the vicinity of the shrine. People who do not approve of the slaughter of animals cut off the right ear of a goat or sheep and, after carrying it round the temple, offer it to the pūjārī. The blood of animals offered in sacrifice in Bellary is not sprinkled round either the shrine or the town. People who offer animal sacrifices also offer boiled rice with them. The rice is heaped on leaves in front of the shrine, turmeric and kunkuma are sprinkled over it, and then it is distributed to the people present. Tuesdays and Fridays are regarded as specially suitable days for the worship of this deity and are observed as days of fasting by the pūjāris of the shrine.

About February every year the hook-swinging festival is celebrated in connexion with the worship of Durgamma.[1] Originally devotees swung from the top of a high pole by hooks fastened through the muscles of their backs; but in these days only an effigy is swung from the pole. It is quite common, however, for devotees to come to the shrine with silver pins fastened through their cheeks. These pins are about six inches long, and rectangular in shape. They are thrust through both cheeks, and then fastened, just like a safety-pin. The devotee comes to the temple with his cheeks pierced in this fashion, and with a lighted lamp in a brass dish on his head. On his arrival before the shrine, the lamp is placed on the ground, and the pin removed and offered to the goddess. I was told that the object of this ceremony is to enable the devotee to come to the shrine with a concentrated mind!

It was also formerly the custom for women to come to the shrine clad only in twigs of the margosa tree, prostrate themselves before the goddess, and then resume their normal clothing. But this is now only done by children, the grown-up women putting the margosa branches over a cloth wrapped round their loins.

The ceremonies performed in the Mysore State, further south, do not materially differ from those already described, though they seem in some places to have been greatly influenced by sun-worship.

Bangalore. In Bangalore there is a shrine of Maheśvaramma, at a village near the Maharajah's palace. The popularity of the shrine seems to have declined in recent years, but daily offerings of fruit and flowers, camphor and incense are still made, and on Tuesdays and Fridays people sometimes bring fowls and sheep to offer to the goddess. When there has been illness in a house, or when, for some other reason, special vows have been made, women often come to the shrine with a silver safety-pin thrust through their cheeks, as is

[1] See p. 59, n. 1, above.

PLATE XI

SHRINE OF PLAGUE-AMMA, BANGALORE

PLATE XII

INTERIOR OF SHRINE OF PLAGUE-AMMA, BANGALORE

the custom for men at Bellary. They offer fruit and flowers, prostrate themselves on the ground before the image, then take out the pin and present it to the goddess.

In front of the shrine, in an open space across the road, about fifteen yards off, stands a block of granite like a thick milestone rounded above, with a small hollow on the top, and a female figure without arms, representing Doddamma, the sister and companion of Maheśvaramma. The pūjārī pours the curds they bring into the hollow on the top of the stone, and smears the image with turmeric and kunkuma, puts a garland round the stone and breaks a cocoanut before it. Doddamma seems to be treated as a younger sister of the goddess, whom it is politic to propitiate, though with inferior honours.

An annual festival is held in this village after harvest. A special clay image is made by the goldsmith from the mud of the village tank and a canopy is erected in a spot where four lanes meet, and decorated with tinsel and flowers. The goldsmith takes the image from his house, and deposits it beneath the canopy. The festival lasts three days. On the first day the proceedings begin at about two p.m., the washerman acting as pūjārī. He is given about two seers of rice, which he boils, and at about five p.m. brings and spreads before the image. Then he pours curds and turmeric over the image, probably to avert the evil eye, and prostrates himself. The villagers next bring rice, fruits, flowers, incense and camphor, and *ārati*, *i.e.* small lamps made of rice-flour paste, each with oil in it and a lighted wick. These are very commonly used in the Canarese country. One āratī is waved by the head of each household before the clay image, another before the shrine of Maheśvaramma, another before a shrine of Muneśvara about two furlongs off, and a fourth at home to his own household deity. During these ceremonies music is played, and tom-toms are sounded without ceasing. After this ceremony any Śūdras, who have made vows, kill sheep and fowls in their own homes and then feast on them, while the women pierce their cheeks with silver pins, and go to worship at the shrine of Maheśvaramma. At about nine p.m. the Mādigās, who are esteemed the left-hand section of the Outcastes, come and sacrifice a male buffalo, called *devara kona*, *i.e.* consecrated buffalo, which has been bought by subscription and left to roam free about the village under the charge of the *Toti*, or village watchman. On the day of the sacrifice it is brought before the image, and the Toti cuts off its head with the sacrificial chopper. The right foreleg is also cut off and put crosswise in the mouth, and the head is then put before the image with an earthen lamp alight on the top of it. The blood is cleaned up by the sweepers at once, to allow the other villagers to approach the spot; but the head remains there facing the image till the festival is over. The Mādigās take away the carcass and hold a feast in their quarter of the village.

On the second day there are no public offerings, but each household makes a feast and feeds as many people as it can. On the third day there is, first, a procession of the image of Maheśvaramma, seated on her wooden horse, and that of Muneśvara from the neighbouring shrine, round the village. They stop at each house, and the people offer fruits and flowers but no animals.

At about five p.m. the washerman takes up the clay image of the grāma-devatā, goes with it in procession to the tank, accompanied by all the people, to the sound of pipes and tom-toms, walks into the tank about knee-deep, and there deposits the image and leaves it.

Kempapura Agrahāra. This is the common type of festival held in honour of the grāma-devatā in all the villages round about Bangalore, whatever special deity may be worshipped, allowing, of course, for the variations of detail which are found everywhere. In one small village with a big name, *viz.* Kempapura Agrahāra, where Pūjamma is worshipped, the pūjārī of the shrine has nothing to do with the buffalo sacrifice during the annual festival. That ceremony is performed by the Mādigās alone. The blood of this victim is mixed with some boiled rice in a large earthen pot, and taken at night round the village by the Toti, and sprinkled on the ground. The Mādigās go with him carrying torches and beating tom-toms. The object of this ceremony is, as usual, to keep off evil spirits.

Yelahañka. Pūjamma is especially the goddess of the Mādigās in these parts, and the buffalo sacrifice forms an important part of the annual festival whenever she is worshipped. At a group of villages some ten miles from Bangalore, near Yelahañka, I found that she was represented by no image, but by a small earthen lamp, which is always kept lighted.

Shrine near Bangalore. At one shrine on the outskirts of Bangalore, where there are seven goddesses, *viz.* Annamma, the presiding goddess, Chandeśvaramma, Māyeśvaramma, Maramma (the goddess of cholera), Udalamma (goddess of swollen necks), Kokkalamma (goddess of coughs), and Sukhajamma (goddess of small-pox and measles), the fire-walking ceremony forms an important part of the annual festival, which lasts for ten days. A trench is dug in front of the shrine about thirty feet long, five feet wide and one-and-a-half feet deep, and washed with a solution of cow-dung, to purify it. About thirty seers of boiled rice are then brought on the fifth day of the festival, and offered to the goddess before the trench. It is all put into the trench and some ten seers of curds are poured over it and then distributed to the people, who eat some on the spot and some at home. A cartload of firewood is then spread over the trench, set alight and left to burn for about three hours, till the wood becomes a mass of red-hot embers. When all is ready, the people assemble, and the pūjārī, whose turn it is to conduct the worship, first bathes to purify himself, and then, amid the deafening din of trumpets, tom-toms, and cymbals, and the clapping of hands, walks with bare feet slowly and deliberately over the glowing embers the whole length of the trench towards the shrine of the seven goddesses. After him about thirty or forty women walk over the red-hot embers with lighted āratīs on their heads. Such is the power of the goddess, the people told me, that no one is injured. The pūjārī of the shrine declared positively that the people put no oil nor anything else on their feet when they walk over.

Mysore City. At Mysore City, where the fire-walking ceremony is also performed, I asked three men who had walked over the trench why they were not hurt, and their reply was that people who were without sin were never hurt! I can only say that in this case their faces sadly belied their characters.

The following account of the worship of village deities in the City of Mysore, and the note on the worship of village deities in the Canarese country generally, was kindly given to me by the late Mr. Ramakrishna Rao, then palace officer at Mysore:

The Maris of Mysore are said to be seven in number, and all the seven are sisters:

(1) Bisal Mari (the sun);
(2) Goonal Mari;
(3) Kel Mari (the earthen pot);
(4) Yeeranagere Mari;
(5) Hiridevathi (the eldest sister);
(6) Chammandamma;
(7) Uttahnahaliamma.

Of the seven Maris, Hiridevathi is said to be the eldest. Every year the Mari Jatra (*i.e.* festival) is held, generally in the month of February. It lasts for about four weeks, and consists of the following:

(1) Mari Saru;
(2) Mari Made;
(3) Mari Sidi;
(4) Kelammana Habba;

each taking nearly a week's time.

(1) *Mari Saru*. On Sunday of the first week of the Mari Jatra, at about six p.m., the people and pūjārīs, called Toreyars, collect at a consecrated place in the fort (the place now used is a little to the east of the southern entrance to the palace), cook rice there, and colour the cooked rice red with the blood of a sheep or

Plate XIII

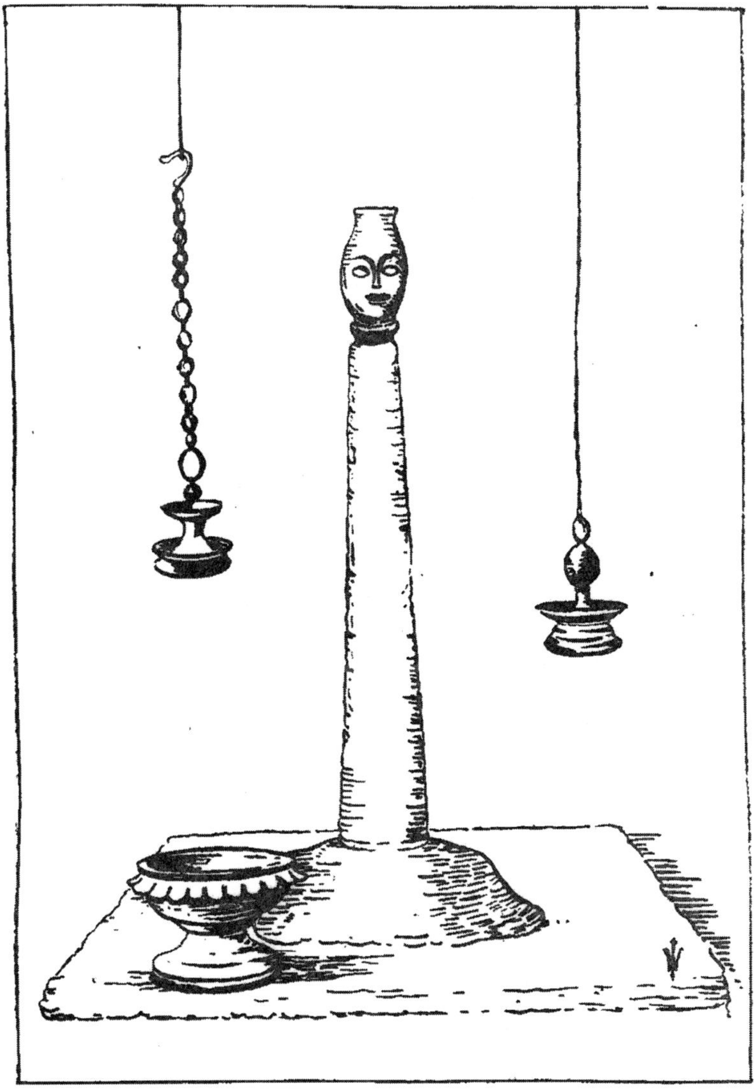

IMAGE OF HULIAMMA IN VILLAGE NEAR MYSORE CITY

Plate XIV

IMAGE OF GODDESS, WORSHIPPED ESPECIALLY BY THE GOLDSMITHS OF MYSORE CITY

goat killed on the spot. After offering the rice to the Bisal Mari they take it, with the carcass of the goat, to the south fort gate and westwards, going round the fort in the inner circle, dragging the carcass of the goat on the ground, and all the way sprinkling the red rice over the streets (this is said to purifv the place lying inside the circle traced in their course), till they arrive at the point whence they started. They then convey the carcass and the remaining rice to a spot near the shrine of Madeśvara, situated in the quarters where they live. Then the entrails of the goat are roasted and, with the rice, divided into three equal parts, and made into three balls, which are given away to the *Chakras*[1] for their services in tom-toming during the rice-sprinkling ceremony.

(2) *Mari Made.* On Monday of the second week the Toreyars throw away all their old earthen pots, used for cooking, and get their houses whitewashed. They get new pots, prepare *Kitchadi*[2] in them, cover them with earthen lids and put āratīs on them. At about six p.m. the āratīs are carried by females to a consecrated pial (platform) known as the Gaddige, and placed in front of a Kunna Kannadi (a looking-glass used as a symbol of the goddess). Two sheep or goats are killed in sacrifice on the spot, and all the flesh is distributed amongst the families of Toreyars. This done, the Kitchadi pots are carried by females in procession to the Bisal Mari shrine, cloths about four feet wide being spread all along the way on which the procession walks, that they may not tread on the earth. The Kitchadi in all the pots is offered to the Bisal Mari, and heaped up on a cloth in front of the Bisal Mari image. The females return home with the empty pots, which will henceforth be used for cooking in their families. The heap of Kitchadi then becomes the property of the washerman Pūjārī, who distributes it amongst his friends and relatives. At the end of this

[1] A section of the Outcastes.
[2] A dish of flour and buttermilk.

week the Mane Manchi shrine, which remains closed all the year, is opened. It contains a hole resembling an ant-hill, which is said to be the abode of an unknown serpent, to which the name of Mane Manchamma is given. Prayers are offered here, chiefly by the men that are to swing on the Sidi, but also by the man that performs the "Human Sacrifice Ceremony," which is now a semblance, not a reality. The Toreyar caste men generally bring from their houses bunches of plantains and store them in this shrine. They are placed there to remain till the Sidi is over, after which they become the property of the families by whom they were brought to the shrine.

(3) *Mari Sidi*. This occupies the third week of the Jatra. On the Sunday before the Monday on which the Sidi takes place, the Human Sacrifice Ceremony called *Bali* (Sanskrit for offering) is performed. It begins at midnight, and lasts till dawn. The man appointed for the Bali is made to lie down, a piece of cloth fully covering his body. This takes place on the same spot where the rice for the Mari Saru (already explained) was prepared. A carpenter begins the ceremony by touching the man lying down with a cluster of flowers of the cocoanut tree. The Chakras[1] keep tom-toming, while the carpenter dances round the victim, singing songs. Fires are lit all round. The carpenter closes his dance by touching the victim again with his cluster of flowers about daybreak. The people present carry the victim (the Bali man) to the Mane Manchi shrine, where he takes rest and walks straight home.

On Monday the carpenter who performed the Bali ceremony the previous day gets the Sidi Car fitted up. It is ready about five p.m. for the swing. The men to swing[2] on the Sidi are kept without food. They take a cold bath, dress themselves on the pial of Gaddige (mentioned in connexion with Made[3]) and then go to the palace, where they get a pre-

[1] See p. 81, n. 1. [2] See p. 59, n. 1. [3] See p. 81.

Plate XV

SHRINE OF POLERAMMA

SHRINE AND IMAGES OF BISAL-MARI

PLATE XVI

IMAGES OF BISAL-MARI

sent of some betel leaves and nuts, and thence they proceed to the shrine of Mane Manchi, offer prayers there, and join the party in Bisal Mariamma-nagudi, *i.e.* the temple of Bisal Mari, where the Sidi is ready with the victims, *viz.* two buffaloes, one on behalf of each man that swings on the Sidi, and a sheep or a goat. The buffaloes are smeared with turmeric (yellow powder) and kunkuma (red powder), and are also garlanded with flowers and margosa leaves. They remain with the Sidi, but, before the men are allowed by the carpenter to swing on the Sidi, the carpenter tests his fittings, and offers the goat in sacrifice. Its blood is taken and sprinkled over all the joints of the car and the wheels of the Sidi. The goat sacrificed is given away to the coolies that work at the car. Then the Sidi procession begins. The two men who are to swing go with the buffaloes to the Hiridevathi shrine, where another Sidi party from Yeerangere, the northern part of the city, meets them with another Sidi, one buffalo, and one man to swing. One at a time mounts on each Sidi. After mounting, each lightly strikes the other as the Sidis cross. Then each swings suspended by a band round his waist on his Sidi. It is at this time that the buffaloes are all killed one after another. It is attempted to cut off the head of each victim with one blow, but actually more blows are used before the buffaloes' heads are severed. When this is over, the men on the Sidis get down and return to the Hiridevathi shrine. There they offer pūjā, after which the parties return home. The party from the Bisal Mari shrine go to the Mane Manchi shrine, take rest, dine, and spend the night there, offering prayers, etc. The following morning they walk home.

(4) *Kelammana Habba.* The same night the buffaloes' carcasses are removed by Chakras and carried to the open place outside the fort, adjoining the southern wall, forming the Barr Parade Maidan, which place is presumed to be that of Kel Mari. There they put up for the occasion a green shed, and place the two buffaloes' heads within it. On these heads are placed lights, and

the faces are smeared with fat turmeric, and kunkuma. The right foreleg of each animal is cut off, and stuck into the mouth. The flesh, etc., of the buffaloes is cooked and eaten by the Chakras as well as by their friends and relatives. For one week the heads are kept in the above sheds and worshipped every day. On the next Monday the Chakras and Holeyars, called also the Balagai caste, carry the heads of the two buffaloes in grand procession to their quarters and eat them up, if they are not very putrid.

A legend is prevalent regarding this Kel Mari. Hiridevathi, the eldest of the Mari sisters, is said to have ordered one of her younger sisters, Kel Mari, to bring fire. The latter went, and in her search for fire she found a lot of low-caste men cooking the flesh of a buffalo and eating the same. It was a curious sight for her to see them do so. She sat there observing what was going on, and lost time. As she was late, the eldest sister was very angry and excommunicated her with a curse, saying that she should only be worshipped by the lowest class of people. Hence the heads of the buffaloes are worshipped in the name of Kel Mari.

The following legend is believed by the common people. Once upon a time there lived a Ṛishi who had a fair daughter. A Chaṇḍāla, *i.e.* an Outcaste, desired to marry her. He went to Kāsī (Benares) in the disguise of a Brāhman, where, under the tuition of a learned Brāhman, he became well versed in the *śastras* (*i.e.* the sacred books), and learnt the Brāhman modes of life. On his return he passed himself off for a Brāhman, and after some time made offers to the Ṛishi lady, and somehow succeeded in prevailing upon her to marry him. She did so, her father also consenting to the match. They lived a married life for some time, and had children. One day it so happened that one of the children noticed the father stitch an old shoe previous to going out for a bath. This seemed curious, and the child drew the mother's attention to it. Then the mother, by virtue of her *tapas* (*i.e.* austerities), came to know the base trick that had been played upon her by her husband, and cursed him and herself. The curse on herself was that she should be born a Mari, to be worshipped only by low-caste men. The curse on him was that he should be born a buffalo, fit to be sacrificed to her, and that her children should be born as sheep and chickens. Therefore, during the periodical Mari festivals, buffaloes, sheep, and chickens are used as victims, and the right leg of the male buffalo is cut off and stuck in his mouth, in memory of his having stitched the shoes in his disguise as a Brāhman.

Animal sacrifices are generally offered by Vaiśyas and Śūdras, the victims being usually buffaloes, sheep or goats, and fowls. These sacrifices are usually propitiatory. Sometimes they are thank-offerings, but there is no sin-offering. When, owing to sickness, any one's life is despaired of, a vow to sacrifice the life of an animal on the recovery of the sick person is made and carried out by the convalescent as soon as possible after restoration to health. Should any misfortune happen to a personal enemy, an animal is at once sacrificed as a thank-offering!

In all these cases, the victim is taken before the altar, and there decapitated by a stroke of a sword, the blood being sprinkled on the object before which the sacrifice is offered, or on the ground in the vicinity. In no case is the blood ever sprinkled on the persons offering the sacrifice. Before a building is finished or occupied, the same kind of sacrifice is made, to propitiate the spirit supposed to have already entered there, and the blood of the victim is sprinkled over the materials of which the building is constructed.

Similarly, when a well is sunk, or a tank built, or a new tool or agricultural implement used, all of which from their nature might be the means of causing death, a sacrifice is offered to the evil spirit to prevent accidents, and, in the case of sharp-edged tools, blood is poured on that part which would cause the hurt. A partial sacrifice is made in the case of tools and implements which from their nature would not be likely to cause death, and in these cases only a slight cut is made, usually in the nose or ear of the animal, sufficient to draw a few drops of blood, which are smeared on the tool, as already mentioned. In cases of epidemics, blood is poured over the image of the deity supposed to be responsible for the disease.

Coorg. The relic of human sacrifice described above, in Mr. Ramakrishna Row's memorandum, would serve to show that in Mysore such sacrifices, at one time, formed a regular part of the worship of the village deities; and this is confirmed by the account given in the *Mysore and Coorg Manual* by Mr. Lewis Rice[1] of the worship of the grāma-devatā in Coorg, which is a hill country to the west of the Mysore State inhabited by a mixed population consisting of aboriginal tribes, a hundred and twenty thousand cultivators and artisans, who were formerly serfs but are now freemen, and a ruling class of Kodagas or Coorgs, who probably migrated into the country about the third century A.D. He writes:

"The essential features of the religion of the Coorgs are anti-Brāhmanical, and consist of ancestral and demon-worship. As among other Dravidian mountain tribes, so also in Coorg, tradition relates that human sacrifices were offered in former times to secure the favour of their grāma-devatās, Mariamma, Durgā, and Bhadra-Kālī,[2] the tutelary goddesses of the Śakti[3] line, who are supposed to protect the villages or Nāds from all evil influences. In Kirindadu and Koniucheri-Grāma in Katiyet Nād, once every three years, in December and June, a human sacrifice used to be brought to Bhadra-Kālī, and during the offering by the *panikas* (a class of religious mendicants), the people exclaimed 'Al Amma!'—'A man, oh mother!'—but once a devotee shouted 'Al All Amma, Adu!'—'Not a man, oh mother! a goat'; and since that time a he-goat without blemish

[1] Vol. iii, pp. 264, 265.
[2] Durgā and Bhadra-Kālī are names of Kālī, the wife of Siva.
[3] See above, p. 29, n. 1.

has been sacrificed. Similarly in Bellur in Tavaligeri-Murnad of Kiggatnad taluq, once a year, by turns from each house, a man was sacrificed by cutting off his head at the temple; but when the turn came to a certain home, the devoted victim made his escape into the jungle. The villagers, after an unsuccessful search, returned to the temple, and said to the pūjārī 'Kalak Adu,' which has a double meaning, *viz.* Kalak, next year, Adu, we will give, or Adu, a goat, and thenceforth only scapegoats were offered. The devotees fast during the day. The he-goat is killed in the afternoon; the blood is sprinkled upon a stone, and the flesh eaten. At night the Panikas, dressed in red and white striped cotton cloths, and their faces covered with metal or bark masks, perform their demoniacal dances. In Mercara taluq in Ippanivolavade, and in Kadikeri in Halerinad, the villagers sacrifice a Kona or male buffalo instead of a man. Tied to a tree in a gloomy grove near the temple, the beast is killed by a Mēda (a wandering tribe, who are basket and mat makers), who cuts off its head with a large knife, but no Coorgs are present at the time. The blood is spilled on a stone under a tree, and the flesh eaten by the Mēdas. In connexion with this sacrifice there are peculiar dances performed by the Coorgs around the temple, the *kombata* or horn dance, each man wearing the horns of a spotted deer or stag on his head; the *pili-ata* or peacock's feather dance, the performers being ornamented with peacock's feathers, and the *chauri-ata* or yak-tail dance, during which the dancers, keeping time, swing yak-tails. These ornaments belong to the temple, where they are kept.

"In some cases where a particular curse, which can only be removed by an extraordinary sacrifice, is said by the Kaniya[1] to rest upon a house, stable, or field, the ceremony performed seems to be another relic of human sacrifices. The Kaniya sends for some

[1] The Kaniyas are religious mendicants, said to be descendants of a Malayalī Brāhman and a low-caste woman.

of his fraternity, the Panikas or Bannus, and they set to work. A pit is dug in the middle room of the house, or in the yard or the stable, or the field, as the occasion may require. Into this one of the magicians descends. He sits down in Hindu fashion muttering mantrams. Pieces of wood are laid across the pit, and covered with earth a foot or two deep. Upon this platform a fire of jack wood is kindled, into which butter, sugar, different kinds of grain, etc., are thrown. This sacrifice continues all night, the Panika sacrificer above, and his immured colleague below, repeating their incantations all the while. In the morning the pit is opened, and the man returns to the light of day. These sacrifices are called *maranada bali*, or death atonements. They cost from ten to fifteen rupees. Instead of a human being, a cock is sometimes shut up in the pit and killed afterwards.

"In cases of sore affliction befalling a whole Grāma or Nād (village), such as small-pox, cholera, or cattle disease, the ryots combine to appease the wrath of Mariamma by collecting contributions of pigs, fowls, rice, cocoanuts, bread, and plantains from the different houses, and depositing them at the *Mandu*: whence they are carried in procession with tom-toms. In one basket there is some rice, and the members of each house on coming out bring a little rice in the hand, and waving it round the head, throw it into the basket, with the belief that the dreaded evil will depart with the rice. At last the offerings are put down on the Nād boundary, the animals are killed, their blood is offered on a stone, the rice and basket are left, and the rest of the provisions are consumed by the persons composing the procession. The people of adjoining Grāmas or Nāds repeat the same ceremony, and thus the epidemic is supposed to be banished from the country. In still greater calamities, a flock of sheep is driven from Nād to Nād, and at last expelled from the country."

CHAPTER VI

MODES OF WORSHIP IN THE TAMIL COUNTRY

The ceremonies observed in the worship of village deities in the Tamil districts of Tanjore, Trichinopoly, and Cuddalore closely resemble those prevailing in the Telugu and Canarese countries; but there are striking differences, which seem largely due to the influence of Brāhmanical ideas and forms of worship. In the first place the ceremonial washing of the images and the processions during the festivals are much more elaborate in these districts than among the Telugus and Canarese. Then, again, the male deities connected with the goddesses are much more prominent, and tend much more to assume an independent position. Iyenar is entirely independent and has a separate shrine and often a separate festival, while in many cases special sacrifices are made to the male attendants, Madurai-Vīran and Munadian. And then, in the third place, there is a widespread idea that animal sacrifices are distasteful to good and respectable deities, both male and female, so that no animal sacrifices are ever offered to Iyenar or to the good and kind goddesses. The ancient sacrifices of fowls, sheep, goats, and buffaloes are, indeed, still offered, but only to the male attendants, Madurai-Vīran and Munadian, and not the goddesses themselves; and while the animals are being killed a curtain is often drawn in front of the image of the goddess, or else the door of her shrine is shut, lest she should be shocked at the sight of the shedding of blood.

An account of the modes of worship and festivals in some typical villages will clearly show both the resemblances to the Telugu and Canarese uses, and also the striking differences.

Vandipaliam, Cuddalore District. In the district of Cuddalore, at a village called Vandipaliam, three deities are worshipped, Mariamman, Draupati and Iyenar, each of whom has a separate shrine. Mariamman's is the largest, about twelve feet high, twenty-five feet long, and twelve or fifteen feet broad. Draupati's is less imposing, being only about six feet high, ten feet long, and eight feet broad.

Iyenar stands in the open, under a tree, with clay images of horses, elephants, dogs, and warriors (or Vīrans) on either side. The Vīrans are supposed to keep watch over their master, while the animals serve as his *vāhanams*, vehicles, on which he rides in his nightly chase after evil spirits. Individual villagers, both men and women, constantly offer private sacrifices consisting of boiled rice, fruit, sugar, incense, and camphor, or fowls and sheep to the Vīran of Iyenar, and then the victim is brought before the image of the Vīran. Water is sprinkled over it, a wreath of flowers is put round its neck by the pūjārī, and turmeric and kunkuma are smeared on its forehead. Then a bottle of arrack, a pot of toddy, two or three cheroots, some ganja (Indian hemp) and opium, and dried fish are presented to the Vīran, afterwards to be consumed by the pūjārī. Camphor is burnt between the animal and the Vīran, and finally the head of the victim is cut off with a large chopper by a pūjārī, specially appointed for the purpose. Nothing special is done with the blood. The carcass is taken away by the offerer, and the head belongs to the pūjārī who cuts it off.

Once a year a public sacrifice is offered to Iyenar by the whole village, some time in April or May. On this occasion the image of Iyenar, which is made of granite and stands about one-and-a-half feet high, is first washed with gingelly oil,[1] lime-juice, milk and curds, with

[1] Gingelly is an Indian name for *Sesamum Indicum* and *Sesamum Orientale*.

cocoanut, plantains, sugar, and some aromatic spices all mixed together.[1] Then cocoanut milk and sandalwood paste are put on the forehead, and a cloth tied round its waist. The villagers bring boiled rice, cocoanuts, plantains, betel leaves and betel nut, sweet cakes of rice, flour, sugar and cocoanut in large quantities, and spread them all on leaves upon the ground before the image. The pūjārī burns incense and camphor, and finally the offerings are all distributed among the people present. After these offerings have been duly made, a curtain is drawn in front of the image of Iyenar, and sheep and fowls are sacrificed to the Vīran, in the same way as at private sacrifices.

Mariamman and Draupati have each one annual festival, which lasts for ten days, but no animal sacrifices are ever offered on these festivals, or on any other occasions at the shrines of these goddesses. The festival begins with the hoisting of a flag, and then for eight days there are processions morning and evening, when a metal image of the goddess is carried in a palanquin through all the streets of the village. On the ninth day there is a car procession, when the image is put on a large car, about twenty feet high, and dragged round the village, while on the night of the tenth day the image is put on a raft and dragged round the tank with torches, pipes, and tom-toms.[2] Offerings of boiled rice, fruits and flowers, incense and camphor, are made every day, and especially on the ninth day, when a large crowd usually assembles.

Shiyali, Tanjore District. At a large village in the Tanjore district, named Shiyali, where Brāhmanism is very strong, Iyenar, Pidāri, Mariamman, Aṅgalamman, and Kālīamman are all worshipped with typical rites; but in this village, though no animal sacrifices are offered to Kālīamman, Mariamman, Pidāri or Aṅgalamman, yet they are offered to the subordinate male deities,

[1] These ablutions are copied from the great temples.

[2] The processions and the progress on the raft are copied from the observances of Brāhmanical temples.

Madurai-Vīran and Munadian, who act as guardians of their shrines. Apparently, however, Pidāri is regarded as slightly less squeamish in the matter of bloodshed than the others, as curtains are drawn before the other three when animals are sacrificed to Madurai-Vīran and Munadian, but not before Pidāri. No festival is held for Kālīamman, who seems to be a rather inert deity, of no great account in practical affairs.

During the festivals of Mariamman, Pidāri, and Aṅgalamman the ablutions are particularly elaborate. The image is washed twice every day, morning and evening, with water, oil, milk, cocoanut milk, a solution of turmeric, rosewater, a solution of sandalwood, honey, sugar, limes, and a solution of the bark of certain trees, separately in a regular order. This ceremonial washing is called in the Tamil country Abishegam,[1] and certainly deserves an imposing name. The pūjārī next repeats certain *mantrams* (sacred texts) before the image, after the example of Brāhman priests, and the offerings of the people, boiled rice, fruit, flowers, cakes, sugar, etc., are presented, incense and camphor are burnt, and prostrations made to the deity. Every evening, after sunset, an image of the goddess, made of a metal, on a small wooden platform decorated with tinsel and flowers, is carried in procession on the shoulders of the people round the main streets of the village, accompanied with fireworks and torches, and the inspiriting sounds of the tom-tom. After the procession, camphor is burnt, a cocoanut broken, and the image replaced in the shrine.

On the tenth day of the festival, in the evening, animal sacrifices are offered, consisting of fowls and sheep, to Madurai-Vīran and Munadian. People who have made vows, in times of sickness or distress, or in order to secure some boon, bring their victims to the shrine. Water and turmeric are poured on the whole body of the animal, and some mantrams are recited by

[1] *Abhisheka*, the Sanskrit word for the ceremonial anointing of a king or a god.

the pūjārī. If the animal is a sheep or goat, it is then seized by the offerer and his friends, some of whom catch hold of its hind legs, while others hold fast to a rope fastened round its neck, and its head is cut off with one stroke of the chopper by one of the pūjārīs. The head is placed in front of the image of Madurai-Vīran with its right foreleg in its mouth. During the killing of the victim a curtain is drawn in front of Mariamman and Aṅgalamman, but not before Pidāri.

At the festival of Mariamman two special ceremonies are performed, which are not performed at the other festivals in this village, but are quite common elsewhere. When sheep are sacrificed, the blood is collected in earthen vessels, mixed with boiled rice, and then sprinkled in the enclosure of the shrine and in the four corners of the main streets, through which the procession passes. What remains over is taken and thrown away in some field at a little distance from the village.

Then, after the animals have been sacrified, the fire-walking ceremony[1] takes place. A trench is dug inside the enclosure of the shrine and filled with logs of wood, which are set alight and reduced to glowing embers. In the evening the metal image[2] of Mariamman is brought out and held in front of the fire, while a short pūjā is performed by burning camphor. Then the pūjārī walks barefooted over the red-hot embers, followed by other people, who have made vows to perform this act of devotion.

During the festival of Pidāri, there is a car procession on the ninth day, which is always the day of the new moon, and in the evening one or more buffaloes are sacrified to Madurai-Vīran or Munadian. The victim is always a male buffalo, and is generally brought by some private person. Water and turmeric are first poured over it, and it is garlanded with flowers, and then its head is cut off with a single stroke of the chopper by a man of the Paḍayachi caste, who, by the way, is not an Outcaste. The head is placed in front

[1] See p. 79 above. [2] See pp 36-37 above.

of the image, but the foreleg is not cut off or put in the mouth, as is constantly done in the case of buffalo sacrifices in the Telugu country. The blood is collected in an earthen vessel and placed near the image of Pidāri and left there the whole night. Next morning, the people assured me, only a small quantity of blood is found in the vessel, Pidāri having the drunk the greater part of it. The remains are poured away outside the compound of the shrine. The heads and carcasses of the buffaloes sacrificed are all handed over to the Pariahs of the village, who take them away for a feast.

At the festival of Aṅgalamman pigs are sacrified to her male guardians as well as sheep, goats, and fowls, not only by the Pariahs, but also by any caste of Śūdras. The Iyenar festival takes place at the same time as the Pidāri festival, and the same ceremonies are performed, except that no animals are sacrificed at his shrine.

The idea, so naïvely expressed in the Pidāri festival at Shiyali, that the goddess actually drinks the blood of the victims, is not uncommon. In many villages some of the blood is collected in an earthen vessel and placed inside the shrine after the sacrifice. At one village, where pigs are sacrificed to Madurai-Vīran, though the blood is not collected in any vessel, but simply allowed to flow on the ground, the people assured me that Madurai-Vīran drinks it. In the same way the rice and the blood sprinkled through the streets of a village or round the boundaries, which is called poli, or food, in Telugu, is regarded as food for the evil spirits. In many Tamil villages the rice and blood are made up into little balls and thrown up in the air, where, as the people firmly believe, they are seized by the deity to whom the sacrifice is offered, or by the evil spirits that hover round the procession.

Vellore Taluk, North Arcot District. The following interesting descriptions of the invocation of Pidāri and of the karagam procession are quoted from an article by F. J. Richards, Esq., I.C.S.:

"After this part of the cermony is over, the pūjāri

invokes the deity to the accompaniment of a chorus of singers, who are either his relations or who share the income with him. The invocation takes place either near the temple or at some prescribed spot in the direction from which the deity is popularly believed to have arrived at the village. In the latter case, after the abishegam is over, the persons present move in a body to the prescribed spot and then commence the invocation. This invocation, which to the persons present is a period of some anxiety, lasts from ten to thirty minutes, when all on a sudden one of those present gets inspired. The meaning of the invocation is a call to the deity to come and help them in their celebrations. The inspired attentively watches the goddess during the early stages of the worship. Later on, with closed eyes he listens to the song of the pūjārī and his chorus. He goes into a counterfeit slumber, first shutting one eye, then the other, then nodding, then swaying so much to one side that the bystanders have to save him from falling. At last he collapses into the arms of one or more of his neighbours. He is watched very intently by all those present. The attention of the votaries is transferred from the goddess to the inspired man. All those seated around him move away from him, and a space is cleared to enable him to move freely. Camphor is then burnt before him, and the inspired man is moved either to speak or be silent or laugh or weep. The speaking and laughing are welcomed by the votaries with delight. They then ask him to grant them permission for celebrating the festival. Generally the permission is granted when he is either speaking or laughing. But if he should weep or be silent, that is taken as an indication of the wrath of the deity, and fresh songs are sung in louder tones to appease the deity. After a fairly long interval, when all become anxious about their own safety, and when the songs have been well-nigh exhausted, the inspired man is again approached with burning camphor. This time he is generally more sympathetic. Very often he gives his unconditional assent for the celebration of the festival. But occasionally, after according sanction to celebrate the festival, the inspired man lifts up his hand and points at some one whose conduct towards the community might not have been acceptable to them in the previous year. With some reluctance, the man pointed out seeks the forgiveness of the inspired man, and is assured of it on his promising to sacrifice a sheep or a fowl. After permission to celebrate the festival is granted, the people present proceed with the celebration."[1]

"Some years ago, it is said, a horse grazing close by the spot where the goddess had been invoked, got terrified by the noise of the drums, etc., and, after galloping round the temple thrice, stopped in front of the entrance. The villagers attributed the horse's action to the inspiration of the goddess."[2]

On the day of the car procession, which takes place on the second day of the festival, "a well-formed bronze image of the idol is placed in a car immediately after the usual abishegam ceremony, and the car is dragged through the several streets of a village by all the villagers. The pūjārī and the others who wore the kapu on the first day will continue to appear in yellow garments and take active parts in the car procession. The car will generally be preceded by drums and trumpets. In front of the car, one of the villagers who has special pretensions to religious fervour carries the karagam on his head, and entertains the people by vigorous movements to and fro without allowing the karagam to fall. His dress on such occasions consists of loose drawers, which are prevented from slipping by a tape passing round his waist. Generally nowadays a sash is used to keep it in position. The abdomen of this dancer is left open to public view. A piece of square cloth about a yard in diameter protects his back. The right hand holds a long sword and the left hand either a lime or green leaves in a piece of cloth. By pretending to let slip the karagam and by maintaining it in its original place on his head

[1] *Quarterly Journal of the Mythic Society*, Jan., 1920, pp. 111-12.
[2] Ib., p. 119.

he entertains the villagers. Beyond sipping lime-juice he is not allowed to eat or drink anything. As the procession, consisting of drums, the karagam dancer and the goddess in the car, passes through a village, sacrifices are offered to the goddess at all points where two streets cross. The sacrifices in this taluk are fowls on this occasion, owing to the absence of large villages where the people can afford to sacrifice sheep. As the goddess passes through the main streets of a village, at all the houses cocoanuts are broken and incense is burnt. The pūjārī is also given some pecuniary remuneration, but he cannot be sure of it in all villages. He is, however, entitled to retain for his own use the smaller half of the cocoanut presented to him for being offered to the deity. He generally manages to shelve it into a big basket kept by his side for the purpose. The car will go only through the main streets of a village, and will return to its original place of starting without stopping anywhere. It is considered a bad omen amongst the Hindus if the gods and the goddesses have to remain in the streets even for a night in their car. Hence the place of starting must be reached before sunset under any circumstances. The ceremonies for the day will be over when, after reaching the place of starting, a fowl or sheep is sacrificed and the pūjārī and others return homeward. In villages where a so-called 'husband' has been appointed, that person is bound to sleep in the temple, or near its precincts, for this night also. During the night a dramatic performance at the expense of the leading ryots of the village is given. The performance lasts generally from ten p.m. till dawn, and the drama enacted nowadays is a compromise between the rude country dance and the present day dramas."[1]

Essene, Trichinopoly District. Another characteristic festival, which is specially conducted and paid for by the Pariahs, is held in the Trichinopoly district, near the village of Essene, during the month of July or August.

[1] Ib., pp. 114-15.

About a mile south of the village, on the road to Madras, there is a shrine, consisting of a large open enclosure about thirty feet square, surrounded by a low stone wall. On the west side of the enclosure are three large images of men seated on tigers, each about eight feet high, representing Pandur-Karuppanna (Pandur being the name of an ancient village), Padu-Karuppanna (*i.e.* the New Karuppanna), and Ursuthiyan (he who goes round the village); and in front of them a number of small stones, black with oil, six carved roughly into the figures of men and women, and about six quite plain, some of them only about six inches high. At right angles to this row of stones, on the south side, runs a small shrine with seven small female figures representing the *kanimars*, *i.e.* the seven virgins, while at the north-east corner is a small separate enclosure with the figure of Madurai-Vīran on horseback with his two wives seated in front of him. The presiding deities of the shrine are the goddesses, represented by the small stones, and not the imposing but ugly male creatures seated on tigers.

When the time for the festival has been fixed, each family of Pariahs gives about one rupee for the expenses. Then, on the first day, they perform pūjā (worship) in the Pariah street of the village Melakari close by the shrine. Three sets of seven brass pots, standing one above the other, are placed in one of the huts, and on the top of each set a small image made of the five metals, one image representing Padu-Karuppanna, another Pandur-Karuppanna, and the third a female deity, Malaiyayi, who is the wife of Karuppanna. Boiled rice is first offered, cocoanuts are broken and incense burnt to the pots, and then at night there is a sword and spear dance in the compound of the hut.

On the second day the Pariahs come to the shrine, and wash the small black stones and images representing the goddesses, with oil, milk, cocoanut milk, lime-juice, and water, put on them some new pieces of cloth, garland them with flowers, and mark them with sandalwood paste. Then they boil rice on the spot, and offer it to the goddesses, and afterwards bring to the shrine sheep, pigs, and fowls. Water is first poured over each sheep, and, if it shivers, it is accepted by the goddesses; if not, it is rejected.[1] Then one of the Pariah pūjārīs cuts off the head of the acceptable victims with a sword. If the head is cut off at one blow, another pūjārī, who is supposed to be under the influence of the deity, sucks out the blood from the neck of the carcass. During the night he thus sucks the blood of about a hundred sheep. After the sheep have been killed, four or five pigs are offered by a few of the Pariahs, who have made vows. The head of each pig is cut off with a chopper, and then a small quantity of blood is collected in some earthen vessels, newly brought from the potter's house, and placed inside the shrine. When all the people have left the place, the pūjārīs mix this blood with some boiled rice, and throw it about a hundred yards outside the shrine to the north-west, north-east, south-east, and south-west, and that ends the festival.

Trichinopoly. The sucking of the blood is a horrid business, but not so horrid as an annual ceremony which takes place every February or March at Trichinopoly, one of the great centres of trade and education in the Tamil country, during the festival of Kalumaiamman. She is regarded as the guardian against cholera and cattle plague, and epidemics generally. A very fat pūjārī of the Vellāla caste, who holds this unenviable office by hereditary right, is lifted up above the vast crowd on the arms of two men; some two thousand kids are then sacrificed one after the other, the blood of the first eight or ten is collected in a large silver vessel holding about a quart, and handed up to the pūjārī, who drinks it all. Then, as the throat of each kid is cut, the animal is handed up to him, and he sucks or pretends to suck the blood out of the carcass. The belief of the people is that the blood is consumed

[1] See above, p. 55.

by the spirit of Kalumaiamman in the pūjārī; and her image stands on a platform during the ceremony about fifteen yards away.

A similar idea is probably expressed by a particularly revolting method of killing sheep, which is not uncommon in Tamil villages during these festivals. One of the pūjārīs, who is sometimes painted to represent a leopard, flies at the sheep like a wild beast, seizes it by the throat with his teeth, and kills it by biting through the jugular vein.

Irungalur, near Trichinopoly. There is another strange ceremony, which is quite common in the Tamil country, connected with the propitiation of the boundary goddess, where the blood of the victim seems to be regarded as the food of malignant spirits. At Irungalur, a village about fourteen miles from Trichinopoly, it forms the conclusion of the festival of the local goddess Kurumbai. During the first seven days the image is duly washed, offerings of rice and fruit are made, and processions are held through the streets of the village. Then, on the eighth day, a small earthen pot, called the karagam, is prepared at the shrine of the goddess. The elaborate decorations of the karagam have been already described,[1] and I need not describe them again. When it is ready, some boiled rice, fruits, cocoanuts, and incense are first offered to it, and then the pūjārī ties on his wrist a kapu, *i.e.* a cord dyed with yellow turmeric, to protect him from evil spirits. A lamb is next brought and sacrificed in front of him, to give him supernatural power, and he then takes the karagam on his head, marches with it in procession through the village to the sound of tom-toms and pipes, and finally deposits it under a booth erected in the middle of the village. On the eighth, ninth and tenth days the karagam is taken in procession morning and evening, and rice and fruits, camphor and incense are also offered to it.

On the tenth day, at about seven a.m., before the pro-

[1] See p. 37 above.

cession starts, a lamb is killed in front of the karagam. The throat is first cut, and then the head cut off and the blood collected in a new earthen pot filled with boiled rice. The pot is put in a frame of ropes and taken by a pūjārī to a stone, about four feet high, called ellai-kal (*i.e.* boundary-stone), planted in the ground some three hundred yards off. A crowd of villagers run after him with wild yells, but no tom-toms or pipes are played. When he comes to the boundary-stone, he runs round it thrice, and the third time throws the pot over his shoulder behind him on to another smaller stone, about two feet high and some five or six feet in circumference, which stands at the foot of the ellai-kal. The earthen pot is dashed to pieces and the rice and blood scatter over the two stones and all around them. The pūjārī then runs quickly back to the booth, where the karagam stands, without looking behind him, followed by the crowd in dead silence. The man who carries the pot is supposed to be possessed by Kurambai, and is in a frantic state as he runs to the boundary-stone, and has to be held up by some of the crowd, to prevent his falling to the ground. The pouring out of the rice and blood is regarded as a propitiation of an evil spirit residing in the boundary-stone, called Ellai-Karuppu, and of all the evil and malignant spirits of the neighbourhood, who are his attendants. When the pūjārī gets back to the booth, he prostrates himself before the karagam, and all the people do the same. Then they go to bathe in the neighbouring tank, and afterwards return to the booth, when another lamb is sacrificed, and the procession starts off through the village.

In the evening of the same day a pig, a sheep, and a cock are bought from the funds of the shrine, and taken to the shrine itself, which stands outside the village. There they are killed in front of a stone image of Madurai-Vīran, which stands in a separate little shrine in front of that of Kurumbai. A large quantity of rice is boiled inside the walls of the compound, and then the flesh of the three animals is cooked and made into curry. The rice and curry are put on a cloth, spread over straw, in front of the image, while the pūjārī does pūjā to Madurai-Vīran inside his shrine, offering arrack, fruit, flowers, incense, and camphor, and saying mantrams; afterwards, he sprinkles some water on the curry and rice, which are then distributed to the people present. During this sacrifice to Madurai-Vīran Kurumbai's shrine is closed.

Pullambadi, Trichinopoly District. The ceremony of propitiating the spirit of the boundary-stone is very common in the Trichinopoly district, though there are the usual variations of local custom in performing it. At a village called Pullambadi it takes place in connexion with the festival of Kulanthalamman, which lasts for fifteen days. On the first day the image is washed, and a sheep is killed outside the enclosure as a sacrifice to Karuppu (a subordinate male deity), the door of the shrine of the goddess being closed. Rice, fruit, flowers, etc., are also offered to the goddess. On the next six days only rice, fruits, etc., are offered; but on the eighth day two more sheep are sacrificed to Karuppu. From the ninth to the fifteenth day the metal image of the goddess[1] is taken in procession round the village, each day on a different vāhanam:[2] on the fifteenth day it is carried on a car, and on this day three sheep are killed in front of the shrine, before the procession starts, the blood being collected in an earthen pot and mixed with boiled rice. Then a sheep is sacrificed at each of the nine corners of the streets that surround the temple, and the blood of all the sheep is put into earthen vessels by a pūjārī of the Shervagaru caste, called the Kappukaran, the animals being all killed by one of the Pariahs. The Kappukaran then mixes all the blood and rice together in one large earthen pot and carries it to the village, which is about half a mile away. Nine more sheep are sacrificed at nine other corners of the village itself, and their blood is again collected and mixed with the rest. When the car has come back to

[1] See pp. 36-37 above. [2] See p 90 above.

its resting-place and the procession is finished, the Kappukaran takes the large vessel full of blood and rice, and, followed by all the men of the village, some holding him by the arms, goes to the western boundary of the village lands, where is the boundary-stone, ellai-kal, about two feet square and one-and-a-half feet high. A lamb is then killed over the stone, so that its blood flows over it; and the head, which has been cut off, is then placed on the top of the stone. The Kappukaran runs thrice round the stone, carrying the pot full of rice and blood in a framework of ropes, and, facing the stone, dashes the pot against it. This done, he at once runs away, without stopping to look back. The other villagers go away before the pot is broken. This concludes the ceremonies of the festival.

Sembia, near Pudukkottai. At another village, Sembia, in the Pudukkottai taluq,[1] the ceremonies connected with the propitiation of boundary spirits are rather more elaborate. There is a boundary-stone at each of the four corners of the village site, five more stones inside the village, and another stone on the boundary of the village land.

During the Pidāri festival boiled rice, fruits, etc., are offered at all the nine boundary stones in the village. On the sixteenth day the image of Pidāri is taken to the house of the pūjārī, who is to perform the dread ceremony of propitiating the spirits that inhabit the boundary-stone of the village lands. The pūjārī puts the kapu[2] on his wrist, and a goat, entirely black, is sacrificed before the image, and its blood collected in an earthen pot, but not mixed with rice. The metal image of Pidāri is then carried in procession round the village on a wooden horse; and at each of the nine stones in the village itself a lamb is sacrificed. When this procession is ended, the pūjārī with the kapu on his wrist takes the earthen pot, with the blood of the black goat inside it, fastens it inside a frame of ropes, and runs to the

[1] A taluq is a division of a civil district.
[2] See p. 100.

boundary-stone on the extreme limit of the village land. About twenty or thirty villagers run with him, holding him by the arms, as he is out of his senses, being possessed with Pidāri. When he arrives at the stone, he runs once round, and then stands facing it, and dashes the pot against it. Without a moment's delay and without looking behind him, he runs back to the place where Pidāri is seated on the wooden horse, on which she was carried round the village. The image is taken back to the shrine; and the ceremony is at an end.

An untoward event happened a few years ago in connexion with one of these Pidāri festivals, at a village in the Trichinopoly district. The festival had commenced and the pūjārī had tied the kapu on his wrist, when a dispute arose between the trustees of the shrine, which caused the festival to be stopped. The dispute could not be settled, and the festival was suspended for three years, and during all that time there could be no marriages among the Udaya caste, while the poor pūjārī, with the kapu on his wrist, had to remain the whole of the three years in the temple, not daring to go out, lest Pidāri in her wrath should slay him.

Tukanapaliam, Tanjore District. At a village in the Tanjore district, called Tukanapaliam, the boundary spirits are propitiated during the Kālīamman festival by the sacrifice of a buffalo. On the last day of the festival the image of Kālīamman, who in many parts of the Tanjore district is specially the goddess of the boundary, is taken to the boundary-stone, and then one male buffalo is killed beside the stone and buried in a pit close by; but nothing is done either with the head or the blood.

Mahākālīkudi, near Trichinopoly. The worship of the village deity at a village called Mahākālīkudi, about eight miles from Trichinopoly, presents several rather curious features. The chief deity is a goddess called Ujinihoṅkālī or Mahākālī.[1] In her shrine are four subordinate female deities, Elliamman, Pullathal-

[1] Great Kālī.

amman, Vishalakshmiamman, and Aṅgalamman, and three subordinate male deities, Madurai-Vīran, Bathalama, and Iyenar. (This is the only place where I have come across Iyenar as a subordinate deity.) In this temple Ujinihoṅkālī is worshipped by all classes, including the Brāhmans, and while some of the pūjāris are Śūdras, the others are Brāhmans. An old Munsiff of the district told me that he could remember the time when all the pūjāris were Śūdras. The Brāhmans appear to have secured a footing in the shrine about fifty years ago. The yearly festival is held in February or March, and lasts sixteen days.

On the first day, called Kankanadhāranam (*i.e.* the wearing of the bracelet), *kaṅkaṇam*, *i.e.* a gold bangle or bracelet, is prepared for the occasion by the temple authorities and put on the wrist of the image, which is made of the five metals in the form of a woman, and stands about three feet high. This must be done at an auspicious hour either of the day or night. One of the Śūdra pūjārīs at the same time puts a kapu on his own right wrist. Boiled rice, cocoanuts, plantains, and limes are afterwards offered to the goddess, lights are placed all over the shrine, and incense and camphor are burnt. For eight days the same ceremonies are repeated, the same bangle put on the wrist of the image and the same kapu on the wrist of the pūjārī.

On the ninth day this bangle is removed and put in the treasury of the shrine, and a new one put on. The same offerings are made as on the other days, but on this day, for the first time, the image is taken out and carried in procession on a small wooden platform, adorned with tinsel, through the village with music and tom-toms, torches and fireworks.

These ceremonies are then repeated till the end of the festival, but each day, till the fourteenth, the image is carried on a different vehicle or vahanam; on the tenth day on a wooden horse, on the eleventh on a car, on the twelfth on a wooden lion, on the thirteenth in a palanquin, on the fourteenth on a swan or bull. No animal sacrifices are performed during the festival at the shrine itself: but on the eleventh day many sheep and goats are sacrificed in connexion with the car procession. Just after the image is put on the car, a kid is brought in front of it and decapitated by a village watchman, or *kavalgar*, of the Umbellayar caste. The kavalgar takes up the head and carcass and carries them round the car, letting the blood drip upon the ground, and then gives both to a Pariah servant of the shrine. When the car returns, a sheep is sacrificed in front of it. Its head is cut off by the kavalgar, and its head and body are allowed to lie upon the ground, while fruits, cocoanuts, and camphor are offered. The man who provides the sheep ultimately takes the body and the pūjārī the head. While the car is being dragged through the streets, people who have made vows bring sheep to the doors of their houses, and the kavalgar comes with his heavy chopper and cuts off their heads.

Kannanur, near Trichinopoly. At the neighbouring village of Kannanur there is a curious local variation in the ordinary rite of sacrifice. During the festival of Mariamman many people who have made vows bring sheep, goats, fowls, pigeons, parrots, cows, and calves to the temple, and leave them in the compound alive. At the end of the festival these animals are all sold to a contractor. Two years ago they fetched Rs. 400, a good haul for the temple, which is particularly a large one, covering two acres of ground enclosed by a high wall.

Buffalo sacrifices are not as common in the Tamil as in the Telugu country, but they are offered in many villages, especially in connexion with the worship of Madura-Kālīamman.

Turayur, near Trichinopoly. At a village called Turayur, near Trichinopoly, a buffalo sacrifice is offered once in five or six years. Before the day of the festival is fixed, the chief men of the village go to the shrine, offer rice and fruits, etc., and ask the goddess whether they may perform the festival. If a lizard utters a chirp in a part of the temple fixed on beforehand, it is taken as a sign that permission is given, and the festival is arranged. The buffaloes devoted for sacrifice are generally chosen some time beforehand by people who make vows in sickness or trouble, and then allowed to roam about the village at will. When they become troublesome, the people go and ask permission of the deity to hold a sacrifice. The buffaloes are brought to the shrine on the appointed day and killed by a man of the Kallar caste, who cuts off the heads with a chopper. Nothing is done with the blood, but both head and carcass are thrown into a pit close by the shrine as soon as the animal is dead. The same pit is used at each festival, but it is cleared out for each occasion. When all the carcasses have been put in, incense and camphor are burnt, cocoanuts and fruits are offered on the edge of the pit, and then earth is thrown in, and the carcasses are covered up. This takes place outside the temple walls, and during the sacrifice a curtain is drawn before the shrine, where the immovable stone image of the goddess is located; but, on the other hand, the metal image, used in processions, is taken out before the sacrifice begins, carried on a wooden lion, and placed on four stone pillars specially erected for the purpose outside the temple, about four or five yards from the place where the buffaloes are killed. No curtain is drawn before this image: the sacrifice is performed in full view of the goddess. It is a curious little compromise between ancient custom and Brāhman prejudice.

Another village. At another village I found that Brāhman ideas had taken one step further in the worship of Madura-Kālīamman, as no animal sacrifices of any kind are offered there to the goddess herself, but only to Periyanna-svāmī, a male deity residing on the top of a hill some three miles away from her shrine; and even there the pūjārīs lamented that, owing to the degeneracy of the age, offerers now take away both head and carcass for their own use, instead of leaving the head, as was done in better days, to be the perquisite of the pūjārīs. At one village I was told that there used to be buffalo sacrifices some twenty years ago; but the people did not know to what deity they were offered, and none are ever offered now.

Pullambadi, Trichinopoly District. At Pullambadi, a village of some size in the Trichinopoly district, I was told that Madura-Kālī only accepts *Vedic*,[1] *i.e.* orthodox, sacrifices. All animal sacrifices, therefore, are made to Madurai-Vīran or Karuppu, her male guardians, and a curtain is drawn before Madura-Kālī while they are being offered. The pūjārī in this village collects the blood of the animals in an earthen pot, mixes it with rice and makes it up into little balls. Then, possessed by Karuppu or Madurai-Vīran, he takes the pot and runs round the temple enclosure, and at each corner throws up a ball of rice and blood, which is carried off by Karuppu or Madurai-Vīran (so the people firmly believe) and never falls down. The Munsiff, who was quite a well-educated man, assured me that this was a fact, and that he had seen it with his own eyes—only, as he admitted, the ceremony takes place in the dark!

Vallum, Tanjore District. Buffaloes are offered in some villages of the Tanjore district both to Kālīamman and Pidāri. Where the sacrifice is strictly performed, as at Vallum, the pūjārī, who is a Śūdra, lives only on milk and fruit, and eats only once a day for a whole month beforehand, and on the day of the sacrifice puts the kapu[2] on his right wrist before he takes hold of the sacrificial sword. It is supposed that he is first inspired by the deity before he can kill the victim. He cuts off the head sometimes in one blow, and sometimes in two or three. Nothing is done with the blood, and both head and carcass are buried in a pit near the shrine. The dung of the victim is mixed with water, and poured over the image of the deity. In some villages in the Tamil country it is customary to take the entrails of the victim and hang them round the pūjārī's neck and put

[1] This word literally means consistent with the Vedas.
[2] See p. 100.

the liver in his mouth during the procession,[1] when the rice and blood is sprinkled through the village, and sometimes part of the entrails is cooked with rice and presented before the image. At one village I found that, after this procession has gone round the houses, it passes on to the burning ghat,[2] where the entrails are taken from the pūjārī's neck and the liver from his mouth; and both are laid down with some curry and rice, which is afterwards eaten by a few of the low-caste people. These extremely repulsive processions, however, are not, as in the Telugu country, especially connected with buffalo sacrifices.

Another village. An unfeeling custom prevails in one village that I came across, which is considerably worse than seething a kid in its mother's milk. When a pig is sacrificed to Aṅgalamman, its neck is first cut slightly at the top and the blood allowed to flow on to some boiled rice placed on a plantain leaf, and then the rice soaked in its own blood is given to the pig to eat. If the pig eats it, the omen is good. If not, the omen is bad. But in any case the pig has its head cut off by a Śūdra pūjārī. In some villages the blood of the pig, offered to Aṅgalamman, is mixed with boiled rice, taken to the burning ghat, where the dead bodies are burned, and thrown into the air at night as an offering to the spirits that hover round the place.

Pudukkottai sub-division, Trichinopoly District. Among other curious applications of the blood of animals, not the least interesting and significant is the one that prevails in nearly all the villages of the Pudukkottai taluq of the Trichinopoly district, where it is the custom for all the villagers to dip cloths in the blood of animals slain simply for food, and hang them up on the eaves of their houses to protect the cattle against disease. This is probably a relic of an age when the eating of animal food under any circumstances had a religious significance.

[1] See above, p. 52, and below, p. 148.
[2] The place where the dead are burned.

Pullambadi, Trichinopoly District. It is refreshing to turn to a custom connected with the worship of village deities which can make some pretence to practical utility. In the village of Pullambadi, at the shrine of Kulanthalamman, whose festival has already been described,[1] an interesting custom prevails, which seems to be not uncommon in those parts. When a creditor cannot recover a debt, he writes out a statement of his claim against his debtor on dried palmyra leaves, presents it to the goddess, and hangs it up on a spear before her image. If the claim is just and the debtor does not pay, it is believed that he will be afflicted with sickness and terrifying dreams, and that in his dreams the goddess will warn him to pay the debt at once. If, however, he disputes the claim, then he in turn writes out his statement of the case and hangs it up on the same spear. The deity then decides which statement is true and afflicts the perjurer with dreams and misfortunes till the false statement is withdrawn. When the claim is acknowledged, the debtor brings the money to the pūjārī, who places it before the goddess, and then sends for the creditor and informs him that the debt is paid. All the money thus paid into the temple coffers is handed over to the various creditors during the festival in April or May, after deducting the amount due to the temple treasury. This is certainly a simple method of doing justice in the matter of debts, and probably just as effective as the more elaborate and more expensive processes of our courts of law. I was told that about ten creditors come to the temple every year, and that the temple had made about Rs. 3,000 as its commission on the debts collected during the last thirty years. Before that time the people came and stated their claims to the goddess orally, promising to give her a share if the debts were recovered; but some thirty years ago the system of written statements was introduced, which, evidently, has proved far more effectual in the settlement of just

[1] See above, p. 102.

claims and much more profitable to the temple. To the practical British mind this seems the one really sensible ceremony connected with the worship of the village deities in South India.

CHAPTER VII

FOLKLORE OF THE VILLAGE GODS OF SOUTH INDIA[1]

A FEW specimens of the folklore connected with the village deities will serve to throw some light on the religious ideas of the people, the antiquity of the village deities themselves, the struggles that have taken place in former years between the worship of these primitive goddesses and the more modern cults of Śiva and Vishṇu, and the efforts made in the later times to connect the ruder village deities with the more dignified gods and goddesses worshipped by the Brāhmans.

Many of the stories are wild and fantastic, marked by a thoroughly Indian extravagance and exaggeration; some seem to be faint echoes of actual events in the past; and many of the details were evidently invented to account for pieces of ritual, the meaning of which had been forgotten. Here is one which probably preserves the traditional story of some palace tragedy and the conversion of the victim into a local deity and also the memory of some attempt made to put down a primitive form of worship.

Mīnāchīamman of Madura. In Madura during the time of the Pandya dynasty, there was a wicked irreligious king called Pandian. In his pride and presumption he closed the temple of Mīnāchīamman,[2] the renowned local goddess. She was enraged at this,

[1] The story of Ammavaru in this chapter is reprinted from an article in the *Nineteenth Century*, by kind permission of the Editor.

[2] Sanskrit, Mīnākshī, fish-eyed, an epithet of the wife of Śiva, probably meaning with love-filled eyes.

and, in order to take vengeance, became incarnate as a new-born infant. King Pandian, who greatly desired to have a child, one day found the deity incarnate as a little girl, lying in the palace, with a very curious bracelet on her arm, which was the exact copy of one belonging to his wife. He wished to adopt the child, but the astrologers warned him that she would bring evil upon his house, so he had her put in a basket and cast into the river. A merchant picked the basket out, brought her up as his own daughter, and called her Kannahai. Shortly before this, it happened that the god Śiva also became incarnate, as another merchant living at Kaveripampatinam, a village at the mouth of the river Kaveri. Hearing of the girl's mysterious origin, he went and married her. After some years he became very poor, and, in spite of his wife's remonstrances, took her strange bracelet to Madura to sell it. It happened that King Pandian's wife had lost her bracelet, which exactly resembled this one, a few days before this. So the merchant was arrested on the charge of stealing it, brought before the king and put to death. In a few days, his wife, Kannahai, went to Madura, heard what had happened, took the form of Thurgai,[1] the demon-killing goddess, and slew Pandian. Since then she has been worshipped by the people. The slaughter of Pandian created in her a desire for bloodshed, and she is now a deity whom it is thought prudent to propitiate.

Madurai-Vīran. The following story is current about Madurai-Vīran in the folklore of South India. He was a soldier in the service of the Naick King of Madura, some centuries ago. The daughter of the king fell in love with him. So Madurai-Vīran gave up his position and all his prospects of promotion and went off with the king's daughter. After their death both Madurai-Vīran and the king's daughter were deified and worshipped. Madurai-Vīran is also known as Patinet-

[1] Durgā, one of the names of Kālī, the wife of Śiva, who got this name because she killed a violent demon named Durga.

tampadi Karuppan, or the guard of the eighteen steps, because, in the courtyard of the Azhagirisami temple, which is one of the richest shrines in all India, there is a flight of eighteen steps, nine of which lead up to a platform on one side while nine lead down from it on the other. On the platform is a huge image of Karuppan, twenty feet high, with enormous eyes as big as umbrellas. The image is covered with spears, guns and arms, which people who have made vows come and offer to Karuppan. The room where the treasures of the temple are kept is locked up every night, and the key, instead of being taken away, is placed on the platform in front of the image. It seems an invitation to burglars ; but nobody would ever dare to take the treasure which is guarded by Karuppan. It is said, in the folklore of the country, that some centuries ago eighteen Māyāvīs, or magicians, so called from the illusion, *māyā*, which they produce in the minds of people, came to the shrine of Azhagiri with the intention of carrying away the essence of the sanctity of the shrine and transporting it elsewhere. Their idea was to carry away the spiritual essence of the god in a wooden cylinder. The god Azhagar, the beautiful one, became aware of the plot to carry away his essence, and so he entered into the body of a small boy, and by his mouth informed the king of the intended outrage and asked him to prevent it. He also told the king that the Māyāvīs would render themselves invisible by a black paste which they put on their foreheads. (This paste is generally made by a distillation of the head of a first-born child that has died, with some other ingredients. If, therefore, a first-born child dies, people generally bury it carefully, in the backyard of their houses, to prevent the head being taken away by magicians for this purpose.) The king consulted Rāmānuja, who was his family priest, and Rāmānuja advised him to shut the doors of the temple and then pour boiling rice-water into the courtyard so that the steam arising from it might melt the paste. This was done, and the Māyāvīs, becoming visible, were arrested by the king's soldiers and put to death, and each one was buried under one of the eighteen steps leading up to the platform on which the image of Karuppan stands, as a solemn warning to all liars and thieves. Civil suits in the Madura district are constantly brought to the temple to be settled by reference to Karuppan. If a man will swear in the presence of the image that his claim is a just one, the claim is admitted to be true, as it is supposed that no one would dare to swear falsely before Karuppan.

One of the many stories current about Mariamma, the goddess of small-pox, is as follows :—One of the nine great Ṛishis in the olden days, named Piruhu, had a wife named Nāgāvalī, equally famed for her beauty and her virtue. One day, when the Ṛishi was away from home, the Trimūrti[1] came to visit her, to see whether she was as beautiful and virtuous as reported. Not knowing who they were, and resenting their intrusion, she had them changed into little children. They naturally took offence, and cursed her, so that her beauty faded away, and her face became dotted with marks like those of the small-pox. When Piruhu returned, and found her thus disfigured, he drove her away, and declared that she should be born a demon in the next world, and cause the spread of a disease, which would make people like herself. In memory of the change which Piruhu found in her, she was called Mari, *i.e.* changed, in the next birth. When she was put away, it is said that a washerwoman took care of her, and that in consequence she was also called Uppai (a washerman's oven). I may remark that a totally different derivation of the word Mari was given me in Mysore.[2]

Another story about the origin of Mariamma is that she was the wife of the Tamil poet Tiruvalluvar, who was a Pariah, that she got small-pox and went from house to house begging for food and fanning herself with margosa leaves to keep off the flies from her sores.

[1] See p. 24, note. [2] See above, p. 29.

When she recovered, the people worshipped her as the goddess of small-pox, and hung up margosa leaves over their doors to keep the small-pox away.

Quite a different story about Mariamma was given me by an Indian Christian, who was told it by his Hindu father. According to this legend, Mariamma was the mother of Paraśurāma, one of the incarnations of Vishṇu, and wife of Jamadagni, a famous Ṛishi (Vedic seer). She was so chaste in mind that she could carry water in a mass without any vessel, and her wet cloth would fly up into the air and remain there till it was dry. One day, as she was coming home from bathing, some of the Gandharvas, or heavenly singers, flew over her, and she saw their reflection in the ball of water in her hand. She could not help admiring their beauty; and, through this slight lapse from the perfect ideal of chastity, she lost her power, the water flowed down to the ground, and her cloth fell from the sky. So she arrived home with no water and with a wet cloth. The Ṛishi questioned her as to the meaning of this and she confessed her fault. Her stern husband ordered her son Paraśurāma to take her into the wilderness and cut off her head. So the son took his mother away, but when they came to the appointed place Mariamma met a Pariah women, and in her longing for sympathy embraced her in her arms. So Paraśurāma cut off both their heads together and went back in great sorrow. His father promised him any reward he chose to ask in return for his obedience: so Paraśurāma asked that his mother might be restored to life. The father granted his request and gave him some water in a vessel and a cane, telling him to put his mother's head on her body, sprinkle the water on her, and tap her with the cane. In his eager haste he put his mother's head on the body of the Pariah woman and *vice versâ*, and restored them both to life. The woman with the Brāhman head and Pariah body was afterwards worshipped as Mariamma; while the woman with the Pariah head and Brāhman body was worshipped as the goddess Yellamma. To Yellamma buffaloes are sacrificed; but to Mariamma goats and cocks, but not buffaloes.

The story is an interesting one, because it probably describes the fusion of the Aryan and Dravidian cults in the days when the Aryans first found their way into South India. A Pariah body with a Brāhman head is an apt description of the cult of Śiva, while a Pariah head with a Brāhman body might well describe some of the cults of the ancient Dravidian deities, modified by Brāhman ideas and influences. The fact that the deity to whom the buffalo is offered was the one with the Pariah head shows that the buffalo sacrifice was specially characteristic of the old Dravidian religion, and suggests that the buffalo was the totem of the Pariahs.

The Buffalo-Sacrifice. Another quaint story, that is found all over the Telugu country in various forms, attempts to account for the prominent part taken by the Pariahs in the worship offered to the village deities, and also to explain some strange features in the ritual. In ancient days, the story runs, there lived a *karṇam*, *i.e.* a village accountant, in a village to the east. He was blind, and had only one daughter. A Pariah, well versed in the Vedas, came to the village in the disguise of a Brāhman. The elders of the village were deceived and induced the blind karṇam to give his daughter to him in marriage, that he might succeed to the office of karṇam in due time. The marriage was celebrated by Brāhman rites, and the karṇam's daughter bore sons and daughters to her Pariah husband, without any suspicion arising in her mind as to his origin. After a time a native of the Pariah's own village came to the place where they were living, and recognized the Pariah disguised as a Brāhman. Seeing, however, that he was a man of influence, he said nothing to the villagers, but went and told the Pariah's old mother. As he was her only son, the old woman set out in search of him, and came to the village where he lived, and sat down by the well used by caste people. The Pariah happened to go there, and recognized his mother; so he took her to a barber, had her head shaved, passed her off as a Brāhman widow, and brought her to his house, telling his wife that she was his mother and was dumb. He took the precaution strictly to enjoin her not to speak, lest her speech should betray them. One day the wife ordered a meal with a dish called Savighai (wheat flour baked with sugar and made into long strings) as a mark of respect to her mother-in-law. During the meal, the mother, forgetting the injunction of silence, asked her son what the Savighai was, saying it looked like the entrails of an animal. The wife overheard the remark, and her suspicions were aroused by the fact that her mother-in-law could speak, when her husband had said that she was dumb, and did not know a common Brāhman dish like Savighai; so she watched their conduct, and felt convinced that they belonged to a low caste, and were not Brāhmans at all. Accordingly, she sent their children to school one day, when her husband was away from home, managed to get rid of the mother-in-law for a few hours, and then set fire to the house and burnt herself alive. By virtue of her great merit in thus expiating the sin she had involuntarily committed, she reappeared in the middle of the village in a divine form, declared that the villagers had done her great wrong by marrying her to a Pariah, and that she would ruin them all. The villagers implored mercy in abject terror. She was appeased by their entreaties, consented to remain in the village as their village goddess, and commanded the villagers to worship her. When she was about to be burnt in the fire, she vowed that her husband should be brought before her and beheaded, that one of his legs should be cut off and put in his mouth, the fat of his stomach put on his head, and a lighted lamp placed on the top of it. (These are details of the buffalo sacrifice, which has been already described, and this part of the story was evidently composed to explain the ritual, of which the true meaning had long been forgotten.) The villagers therefore seized the husband, stripped him naked, took him in procession round the village, beheaded him in her presence, and treated his leg and the fat of his stomach as directed. Then her children came on the scene, violently abused the villagers and village officers, and told them that they were the cause of their mother's death. The deity looked at her children with favour, and declared that they should always be her children, and that without them no worship should be offered to her. The Asādis[1] claim to be descendants of these children, and during the festivals exercise the hereditary privilege of abusing the villagers and village officers in their songs. After being beheaded, the husband was born again as a buffalo, and for this reason a buffalo is offered in sacrifice to Uramma, the village goddess.

A Tragic Tale.[2] Such ceremonies as the buffalo-sacrifice, gruesome as they seem, when witnessed in broad daylight, with the accompaniments of devil-music, bell-ringing and shouting, or rather shrieking, are much more awe-inspiring when seen at night, and are likely to impress a stranger in an unpleasant manner, as the following will show. A—— was a stranger to the country and its ways. He was returning home late one night, guided along his path by the uncertain rays of a young moon. Missing his way, he strayed towards the shrine of the village goddess; and when passing the low walls of the temple his attention was suddenly arrested by a heart-rending moan, seemingly uttered by some one in great distress, inside the walled enclosure. Impelled by thoughts of rendering help to a fellow creature in distress, A—— approached the temple wall, and looking over it, saw the prostrate form of a young and handsome female, of the better class of Hindus, lying motionless as death on the stone pavement. Thoughts of dark intrigues and mysterious murders of a decidedly Eastern type impelled him to climb over the wall; and he was bending over the woman, his hand stretched out in the act of raising up what he believed was the lifeless remains of the victim of some ghastly

[1] See above, p. 44.
[2] This story appeared in the *Madras Mail*.

tragedy, when, quick asligh tning, a gaunt and spectral object, almost nude, bearded to the knee, with head covered by matted tufts of hair and presenting a hideous appearance, emerged from the deep shadows around. The figure held a naked sword in one hand and a bunch of margosa leaves in the other, and bounding up to A——, peremptorily, and with a glance whose meaning could not be mistaken, motioned him away.

A—— was only too glad to retreat as fast as he had come, his enthusiasm not a little chilled; and he leapt over the wall into the pathway, where he met a policeman going his rounds. A—— detained the policeman in order to see the end of the mysterious pantomime that was enacting before the idol, and enquired of him the meaning of the presence there of the woman alone and at that time of night, and of all the rest he saw. He was told that the woman was a matron of a respectable Hindu family, who, having had no children since her marriage, had come, by the advice of her elders, to invoke the assistance of the goddess, as she was credited with the power of making women fertile, and by prayers and offerings prevail on her to make her the mother of a son, and thus save her from the displeasure of her husband, who frequently rated her on her barrenness. The grotesque figure which had so terrified A—— was the village pūjārī, and a noted exorciser of evil spirits; and he was then exercising his art over the terrified woman in attempting to drive away the malignant spirit that possessed her, and had thereby rendered her childless. It is said to be a common belief among many Hindus that barrenness in females is sometimes the result of possession by evil spirits, some of whom have to be propitiated, while others are terrified into leaving their victims. In this case it was a demon of the latter kind, and that accounted for the pūjārī's appearance, in all the majesty and terror of his office as exorcist, sword in hand, to coerce the unwilling one to take his flight.

Just then the woman emitted another blood-curdling shriek, and the pūjārī, coming forward, demanded, in a loud and threatening voice, if the *payee* (devil) had left her. Receiving no reply, he flourished his sword over the prostrate form, muttered some incantations, and struck the woman with the margosa leaves in his hand. He then bade her rise and stand before the idol, which she did in a supplicatory attitude, with head bent and hands crossed, while he proceeded to offer up prayers to the goddess to aid him in driving away the stubborn intruder, after which he bade the woman make her offerings and depart in peace. The woman left the temple staggering, so exhausted had she become under the mental strain to which she had been subjected in the course of the exorcism. A—— had seen Hindu superstition in all its nakedness, and the effect of it had been heightened by every circumstance that could made it awe-inspiring—the sombre shadows of night, the dim flickering of the temple light that threw a ray like a sanctuary lamp, the silence, except when broken by the woman's moans; all helped to impress him deeply.

Frequently, while worshipping at the shrine, it happens that one of the more spiritual of the worshippers becomes possessed of the goddess, and commences to execute the usual devil dance, with dilated eyes, distended nostrils, and a frame suddenly endued with extraordinary activity and strength, proud to act as the mouthpiece of the goddess and to give out her oracles. It not seldom happens also that unscrupulous characters take advantage of this *favouring* by the deity, to impose on the ignorant masses by practising on their credulity. An example of the way in which the deity of an aboriginal family might become a deity of a conquering race and acquire a widespread popularity, is seen in the history of Koniamma in the Coimbatore district. The story goes that at a very remote date, when the tract now occupied by the town of Coimbatore was forest land, inhabited by aboriginal hill-tribes known as Malaisar, *i.e.* dwellers in the mountain, a certain man, named Koyan, who was of some repute among the aborigines, dwelt there and worshipped a goddess who was called after his name, Koyanamma. The name was gradually changed, first into Kovaiamma, and then into Koniamma. After some years she became the village deity of the Malaisar, and a temple was built in her honour, with a stone image of the goddess in front of it. In the course of time, a Hindu king, named Mathe Raja, happened to go there on a hunting expedition, and, finding the spot very fertile, colonized the country with his own subjects. Gradually a flourishing town grew up, and Koniamma was adopted as one of the deities of the new colony. Centuries afterwards, Tippu Sultan, the Tiger of Mysore, when he passed by the town during one of his marches, broke down the image and demolished the temple. The glory of persecution greatly increased the fame of the goddess. The head, which had been broken off the image, was brought back to the town, a new temple built, and in a few years the goddess became very popular over the whole district. Her title to divine honour rests upon the legend that she killed a certain demon, who was devastating the land and took the form of a buffalo when he attacked her. She is regarded as a benevolent being, who does not inflict diseases, but is capable of doing much good to the people when duly honoured. She is worshipped only at Coimbatore. This word is the English form of the Tamil Koyamputhur.

Some of the legends bear witness to the bitter conflict between the aboriginal inhabitants of the land, generally described as demons or *Rakshathas* (Sanskrit *Rakshases*) and the superior races which conquered them, whether Turanian or Aryan.

The legend of Śavadamma, the goddess of the weaver caste in the Coimbatore district, is a case in point. It runs as follows: Once upon a time, when there was fierce conflict between "the men" and the Rakshathas, "the men," who were getting defeated, applied for help to the god Śiva, who sent his wife, Pārvatī,[1] as an avatāra or incarnation, into the world to

[1] Kālī has many names, among which Pārvatī, *i.e.* the mountain goddess, is one of the commonest.

help them. The avatāra enabled them to defeat the Rakshathas; and, as the weaver caste were in the forefront of the battle, she became the goddess of the weavers, and was known in consequence as Śavadamma, a corruption of Sedar Amma, Śedar or Chedar being another title for the weavers. It is said that her original home was in the north of India near the Himalayas.

Another deity, whose worship is confined to a particular caste in South India, and about whom a similar legend is told, is Kanniha Parameśvarī (*i.e.* supreme goddess), the goddess of the Komatis, or traders. The story goes that in ancient days there was bitter hatred between the Komatis, who claim to belong to the Vaiśya[1] caste, and the Mlecchas,[1] or barbarians. When the Komatis were getting worsted in the struggle for supremacy, they requested Pārvatī, the wife of Śiva, to come and deliver them. It so happened that about that time Pārvatī was incarnate as a girl of the Komati caste, who was exceedingly beautiful. The Mlecchas demanded that she should be given in marriage to one of their own people, and the refusal of the Komatis led to severe fighting, in which the Komatis, owing to the presence of the avatāra of Śiva among them, were completely victorious, and almost exterminated their enemies. After their victory, the Komatis entertained doubts as to the chastity of the girl, and compelled her to purify herself by passing through fire. This she did, and disappeared in the fire, resuming her real shape as Pārvatī, and taking her place beside Śiva in heaven. Her last words were a command to the Komatis to worship her, if they wished their caste to prosper.

It will be noticed from these stories that there has been a strong tendency in the Tamil country, where Brāhman influence is strong, to connect the old village deities with the Hindu pantheon, and especially with the god Śiva, the most popular deity in South India. So,

[1] See p. 19 n.

in the Tanjore district, the chief goddesses of the large tribe of village deities are seven sisters, who are regarded as emanating from Pārvatī,[1] the wife of Śiva.

Revenge by Suicide. In the Warangal taluq of the Hyderabad State there are numerous slabs of stone with figures of a man in the act of cutting his throat carved on them in bas-relief. The story goes that in ancient days a king of Warangal promised some Wudders (navvies) a sum of gold for digging a large tank. When they appeared before him for payment, he offered them silver instead; and they went away very sad and angry, and came back again a few days afterwards and all cut their throats in the presence of the king, so that their spirits might haunt and torment him for the rest of his life. They have been worshipped from that day to this, and are among the most popular gods of the district. It was a truly Indian method of taking revenge, and I have often heard of similar acts of retaliation even in modern times.

Basavanna of the Badagas. The following stories, current among the Badagas on the Nilgiri Hills, in South India, may possibly preserve, in a perverted form, the memory of some trivial incidents, which the superstitious fancy of the villagers turned into signs and wonders. The village of Kateri is about ten miles from Ootacamund, and the Kateri falls have been utilized to generate the electric power that now works the Government cordite factory in the broad valley on the other side of the hills. But long before cordite or electric power were thought of, when the Muhammadans ruled in Mysore, one of the villagers of Kateri went down to the plains to pay tribute. When he went to a river to perform pūjā (worship) to a liṅgam, the emblem of the god Śiva, he found on the river bank a stone in the form of an ox. He put it in his pocket, intending to give it to his children as a toy. But when he got home, he forgot all about the stone; and it remained in his pocket till he went down to another river near

[1] See p. 122 n.

Kateri to perform pūjā again. As he came to the bank, he touched his pocket and there found the stone. He took it out, put it down on the bank, and went to do his pūjā. When he came back, it was gone! This greatly astonished him. But when he returned to the river next morning, lo and behold! he saw on the bank the stone turned into a real live ox! Then the ox went off to a neighbouring village, Naduhatty, and there fought with another ox. The owner of this other ox killed the aggressor; but no sooner had he done so, than he turned upside down, and stood on his head with his heels in the air, unable to move. The villagers were filled with astonishment, as well they might be, at this extraordinary conduct; but the man who had found the stone told them that the slaughtered ox was really a god, which he had brought up from the plains, without knowing what it was, to give to his children. The villagers were in great alarm at this; but, when the man returned to his hut, there was the stone figure of the ox, with one of its horns broken and a spear-wound on its left side. The village pūjārī was hastily sent for, and he declared that a daily offering of milk must be made to the stone figure. For some time this was done; then the owner neglected the pūjā, and the stone promptly turned back into a live ox, which attacked the villagers, and would not let any one enter the shed where it stood. The villagers, however, made a hole in the roof, and poured milk upon it from above, and once more it turned into stone, and stands there in the same shed to this day. Warned by the experience of the past, the villagers were careful to make the daily offering of milk, lest it should once more turn into a troublesome ox. The name of the god is Basavanna.[1]

The story reads like a description of a scene from a pantomime, when the harlequin appears on the stage. But it is sober truth to the Badagas of Kateri and the neighbouring villages. It was told to me by the only

[1] *Basava* (Sanskrit *vṛishabha*) stands for bull or ox in the South Indian languages,

Badaga who at that time had matriculated at the Madras University.

Mahāliṅga of the Badagas. Another story current among the Badagas is equally trivial, and is a sample of many local traditions that are current among them. A cow, the story runs, had a calf. She would give no milk, however, for her master, but ran off to a shola (forest) close by his house. He followed her one day, and watched to see why she went there, and saw her go to a stone image and pour over it the milk from her udders. He then went and fetched a spade, and tried to dig the image up, but could not reach the bottom of it; and whenever the spade touched the stone, it drew blood. He went and told the story in the village, so the villagers built a shrine over the image, and worshipped it as the god Mahāliṅga.[1]

Hathay of Paraṅganad. The tradition of the goddess Hathay, *i.e.* grandmother, probably preserves the memory of a real event, as the worship of men or women who have died violent deaths or in a tragic way is common all over South India. About a hundred years ago, a man had a daughter whom he wished to marry to a man in the Paraṅganad division of the Nilgiris. The girl refused, and the father insisted. So at last she went to the village tank (a large pond), sat under a tree, first bathed and then threw herself into the water and was drowned. One of the men in the Paraṅganad division afterwards saw the woman in a dream, and she told him that she was not a human being but a goddess, an incarnation of Pārvatī, the wife of Śiva.

This story illustrates the origin of many deities in India, and also the way in which these local goddesses are tacked on to the religion of the Brāhmans by being made wives, or incarnations of the wife, of Śīva.

Ammavaru, or Aṅkamma. During one of my tours on the East Coast, north of Madras, I got a copy of a manuscript on palm leaves belonging to a village pūjārī

[1] *I.e.* Great Liṅga, the *liṅgă* being Śiva's phallic emblem.

which contains the story of the village goddess Ammavaru, now worshipped as Aṅkamma. The story is recited by the Asādis during the annual festivals. It is a strange, rambling tale, full of weird details, describing the birth of the newer deities, Brahmā, Śiva, and Vishṇu, and the struggle that ensued between the rival religions. It is not improbable that it describes an attempt on the part of the Brāhmans to supplant the worship of the village deity by the new cults and the revival of the primitive religion through some epidemics or other disasters. A bad epidemic of small-pox or cholera, just at the time when the newer forms of worship had caused the old deities to be neglected, would be quite sufficient to revive their popularity and give rise to a fantastic myth describing the event. The myth begins by describing the extreme antiquity of Ammavaru. "Even before the existence of the four Yugas, *i.e.* ages, before the birth of the nine Brāhmans, when sleep did not exist in towns and villages, when the Yugas had no time, before the birth of Maheśvara (*i.e.* great God, a title of Śiva), before the appearance of sky and lightning, before the birth of Gautama Buddha and the sages, before the appearance of Satyasāgara,[1] before the appearance of water reservoirs, such as tanks and lakes, when there were no roads, streets or lanes to towns and villages, before the creation of the world, even before the coming into existence of wells to be defiled by the spittle of fishes, and before the Narayāga[2] Ammavaru came into existence, three eggs were laid by Ammavaru in the sea of milk, one by one in three successive ages. The egg laid first got spoilt, the next filled with air, and only the third was hatched. This egg had three compartments, from which came the Trimūrti,[3] Brahmā, Vishṇu and Śiva. The lower half of the egg was transformed into the earth and the upper half became the sky. The king, who was the avatāra,

[1] Satyasāgara = Ocean of truth.

[2] Narayāga is the term used for human sacrifice; Narayāga Ammavaru is the goddess worshipped by human sacrifice.

[3] See above, p. 24 n.

i.e. incarnation, of Vishṇu, was fed on butter; Brahmā was made to live on turmeric; and Śiva was fed with the milk of Ammavaru. Then, as they grew up, she made each of the gods put on his forehead characteristic religious marks, and finally built three towns, one for each to live in, and a fourth for herself."

This probably preserves a tradition of the relation of the popular Hindu religion of modern days to the older worship of the village deities. It is doubtless true that the Brāhmans gained the victory over their enemies the Buddhists by borrowing largely from the pre-Aryan religions, which had a great hold over the masses of the people. This may be practically expressed by saying that Brahmā, Vishṇu, and Śiva sprang from an egg laid by a village deity, and that she built for them the sacred cities which were the centres of their worship.

The goddess took special pains to protect her own city. She enclosed it with walls of bronze, brass, and gold; posted at the gates several thousand spirits of various sorts, and among them, a barber, a washerman, and a potter. It seems odd to find these humble members of village society in such exalted company; but it is explained by the fact that they are the people who in many parts of South India take a prominent part in the sacrifices offered to the village deities at the annual festivals.

After a time, Ammavaru heard that the three kings, Brahmā, Vishṇu, and Śiva, were neglecting her worship; so she determined to exhibit her power by destroying their towns. Her resolve was strengthened by an insult offered her by Śiva. The god one day called his servant and asked him why the people were neglecting the worship of Ammavaru, and was told in reply that they were calling on his name instead. He then bade his servant go to Ammavaru's town and abuse her, which he did with a will. When she heard of it she smiled grimly, "trimmed her moustaches," and waxed very wroth. She then dressed herself up in a yellow cloth and yellow bodice, put on copper jewels, a silver waistband, and tied a golden ornament on her forehead, took a deer in one hand, a conch in the other, a small drum in a third, and put a snake round her body as a sacred thread.[1] Thus attired, she called a durbar, sat down on the dais, and declared that her pūjā was neglected and she herself abused. After this little speech she started off to Devagiri, the town of Īśvara or Śiva, mounted on a jackal, and accompanied with all kinds of weapons and palanquins. Drums were sounded during the march. The investment of of the town was a quaint proceeding. Besides several kinds of animals, Ammavaru created *Gaṅgā-bhavanī* (a fortified place with a ditch round it) and a sage to conduct the siege. The military operations of the sage were truly original. Seven *rudrāksha*[2] berries were placed on the ground, and on these seven *bhadrākshīs*, *i.e.* a kind of bead in which are marks said to resemble eyes, and on these needles were stuck to support balls of sacred ashes.[3] Through these balls were driven steel spikes which supported a single-headed rudrāksha berry, with seeds of a sacred plant on the top. The sage then put his head on the seeds and raised his legs high up in the air. Birds built their nests on his neck, beetles and bees made their homes in his nose, plants of all kinds grew round him, and cobras made their abode in his arm-pits. He remained silent and spoke to no one.[4] What exactly the purpose or effect of these proceedings was does not appear;

[1] Śiva is often represented holding a deer by the hind legs in one hand and a drum, called *damaru*, in the other; and he frequently has snakes about his neck and waist and in his hair. The conch is one of Vishnu's symbols.

[2] The berry of the *Elaeocarpus Ganitrus* is called *rudrāksha* and is used for making rosaries for the devotees of Śiva.

[3] Śiva is usually represented as covered with sacred ashes, and Śivaite ascetics usually smear their bodies in the same way.

[4] Hindu ascetics practise many austerities, *tapas*. Among the more common forms are long-continued silence and the remaining motionless in one posture until, we are told, beasts, birds, and insects make their resting-place in the man's body. The purpose of these practices is the gaining of boundless miraculous power.

but apparently they were successful, as Ammavaru moved steadily on, and appointed her sister to keep people off the road, and then placed her sisters, the hundred śaktis,[1] to keep watch, and also a twelve-headed snake which coiled its body all round the town, keeping its hooded heads just opposite the gate and emitting poisonous fumes from its mouths. Then, as she went on in her triumphant march, a mountain was put on guard, forts were created, and Ammavaru descended from her jackal and sat on a throne. A horse was then brought her, drums were beaten, what Shakespeare would call alarums and excursions took place, and the sky was turned into a pestle and the earth into a mortar. After this general upset of the universe, Ammavuru made the dumb to sing her praises, created some tents with little demons inside who did pūjā to her, and so finally arrived at Devagiri. Apparently this overwhelming display of military power and science at first crushed all resistance. The heads of the kings (Brahmā, Vishṇu, and Śiva) who refused to worship Ammavaru were cut off, also the heads of seven other kings, and then all put on again! One king's throne was made red-hot like the fire in a potter's kiln, and his hair made all bloody, while demons were set to watch the corpses of the slain. Then Ammavaru afflicted the unhappy citizens with many disasters and started off to attack four other kings. Drums were sounded as before and then a bloody battle ensued outside the walls of Devagiri. Horses and elephants were slain by Ammavaru, one king "felt a bad pain in his chest, as if pierced with arrows, and pains in various parts of his body," and died. Another king took a sword and plunged it into the body of a third king, and both died. Then all the horses and elephants and kings died, and finally Ammavaru brought them all to life again, and they all began to worship her. A year after, drums were sounded again, and she marched with her army to a tamarind tree, where she slept for

[1] See p. 29 n. 1.

seven gadiyas (a gadi = 24 minutes) on a cotton mattress. Then nine kings, who had formerly worshipped Ammavaru, gave up doing so, and changed the Vishṇu marks on their foreheads for those of Śiva. This vexed Ammavaru, so she threatened to annihilate the town of Devagiri and then swooned. When she came to, she took a basket without a rim and some herbs and fruits, transformed herself into an old woman and walked to Devagiri. The watchman of the town refused to help her, put her baskets on her head, threatened to have her beaten, and abused her soundly. She caused a deep sleep to overpower him, tossed her baskets into the air, caught them on her head, and made her way to the gates of the town, which were guarded north, south, east, and west by four huge demons, with ten thousand crores[1] of men holding canes coloured green, and seven hundred crores holding canes coloured red. A number of them were fast asleep; but she roused them up and bade them open the gates, as she wanted to sell her tamarind and jack fruit in the town. One of them got up and told her that baskets with fruits and curds, beggars and mendicants, were not allowed in the town, and added that the people of the town were Liṅgāyats,[2] people of true faith and good character. The goddess shouted, "O Śūdra sisters, living in the east street, O Brāhman sisters of the western street, O Kamma sisters of the southern street, buy fruits from me. Old men eating my fruit will become young and young ones very handsome." The watchman was very angry at this, and beat her with a green cane. The goddess threw down her basket, which caused a great earthquake. Then she first turned into a huge giantess and afterwards into a parrot, and said to the watchman, "You did not recognize me. You have forgotten my might; I will show my power." Ammavaru then disguised herself as a Liṅgāyat dressed in a reddish-brown cloth, took a

[1] A crore is ten millions.

[2] See p. 72 n.

wooden pot in her hand, put sacred ashes on her forehead,[1] tied the symbol of Śiva[2] on every part of her body, sounded bells and conchs, and, saying aloud, "Linga-nama-Śivāya,"[3] approached the gates of Devagiri once more. All the people were amazed at her devotion, prostrated themselves before her and offered a seat, saying, "O worthy woman, where do you come from?" Ammavaru replied, "I am coming from Yatapaliam. My name is Yati-dari-paduchu, and I am coming from Chittangi land. I am alone without relations in the world. I am a happy woman without a husband." "Why do you come to Devagiri?" they asked. Ammavaru replied that during the *krita yuga*,[4] *i.e.* the golden age, Parameśvara (*i.e.* the Supreme, here Siva) became a slave to Pārvatī (wife of Śiva), that he was living in Devagiri, and she had come to pay her respects to him. The gate-keepers refused to admit her till she had told the story of Śiva and Pārvatī. The goddess then told the story as follows: On the wedding-day of Śiva and Pārvatī the gold and silver bracelets were tied to their wrists, pearls were brought from the western ocean, festoons of fig leaves were hung up, and a cloth was stretched as a screen between Śiva and his bride; the faces[5] of Brahmā were covered with sackcloth and twelve Vedas were read: but an inauspicious muhūrtam, *i.e.* moment, was fixed and an inauspicious hour chosen for the ceremony. After tying the *tāli* (a small metal disk or ornament suspended by a thread, the mark of a married woman) round Pārvatī's neck, Śiva put his foot on her foot, and she put her foot on his. Brahmā saw the shadow of Pārvatī's foot, was filled with unholy desires, and disturbed the ceremony by unseemly conduct. Śiva

[1] Śivaites wear sacred ashes smeared on the forehead in three lines. See p. 137.

[2] The phallic symbol, the *linga* whence Lingāyat.

[3] "Reverence to Śiva," the sectarian *mantra*, or watchword.

[4] The Hindus recognize a cycle of four ages, like the Greeks and Romans.

[5] Brahmā i usually represented with four faces

grew very angry, abused Brahmā, and bit off one of his heads. The head fastened on Śiva's hand and remained immovable. So he sent at once for a number of Brāhmans, and asked why he could not get it off They told him that it was because he had committed murder, which is a most heinous crime, and suggested that he should wander about as a beggar, and make pilgrimage to Benares, Rāmeśvaram, and other sacred places, and then receive alms directly from the hands of Lakshmī (the wife of Vishṇu). Śiva then disguised himself as a beggar, and wandered far and wide, and at last came to Lakshmī, and cried out, "O Ādi Lakshmī![1] Alms! Alms!" She ordered her servants to take him alms, but he refused to receive it except at her hands, and said that Lakshmī was his sister. Then Lakshmī bathed, ordered food to be prepared, and served him herself, and at once the skull fell from Śiva's hand to the ground. Śiva began to run away, but the skull begged that some provision might be made for its future existence, as it had lived on his hand for so many years. Lakshmī then waved āratī[2] lights before Śiva, and gave curry and rice to the skull, which promptly fell towards the north and broke in five pieces, murmuring, as it broke that something must be done for it. Śiva replied that it might take hold of pregnant women, women during confinement, and babies, and that this would enable it to obtain worship and offerings.

Ammavaru then related how she herself had desired marriage and gone to Vishṇu, who sent her to Brahmā, who passed her on to Śiva. She danced before Śiva, who promised to grant her wish, if she would give him the three valuable things she possessed—a rug, some betel leaves and a third eye. She gave them all to Śiva, who at once opened the third eye and reduced her to ashes.[3] Then, filled with regret at the rash act,

[1] Ādi means original, existing from the beginning.

[2] See above, p. 39.

[3] Śiva is always represented with a third eye set vertically in his forehead. A Hindu myth tells how he reduced Kāma, the Hindu Cupid, to ashes with one glance of his third eye.

which involved the destruction of all womankind, he collected the ashes and made them into the form of three women, who became the wives of Śiva, Vishṇu, and Brahmā.

After telling this moving story, Ammavaru demanded entrance into the town, when she transformed herself into a parrot and sat on a stone pillar. Many of the inhabitants she caused to faint; on many others she sent fevers and other diseases. Then she flew to the *gopuram*, *i.e.* the towered gateway of the temple, where nine men were worshipping Śiva with his emblem in their hands. Suddenly the emblems became red-hot in their hands, and, dropping them, the nine men cried out, "O Śiva, you are powerless to-day; now we have lost faith in you. Before the moon rises, may your temple be burnt to ashes." Śiva, hearing their cries, came up and threw some sacred ashes over them and touched them with his cane. Then they all got up and said to him, "O Īśvara (*i.e.* Lord), listen to our complaints. We have had enough of your pūjā. Some calamity has befallen us. Give us leave and we will go to our homes." Śiva went off in anger to the gatekeepers and demanded why they had admitted strangers. They replied that they had turned back an old woman selling fruit, and only admitted a Liṅgāyat woman, because she was a devotee. Śiva ordered one of the demons to find her; but Ammavaru transformed herself into a girl of the Velama caste, and mixed with the Velama women in the Brāhman street, and the man looked for her in vain. Then another was ordered to find her; but this time Ammavaru turned herself into a parrot. When the man could not find her, he cried out, "O goddess! Please come! You are the deity of my ancestors. We hear that you have entered our town in the form of a Liṅgāyat." Then Ammavaru asked him what kind of form he meant, saying, "I am your emblem of life." Then the demon felt bad pains all over his body, as though his chest and ribs were broken, rose up high into the air, flapping his hands like wings, caught hold of the parrot and brought her to Śiva.

Śiva complimented the demon on his success, but said that a female deity should not be brought into his presence. He commanded her to be tied to a red-hot pillar of glass and crows with iron beaks to peck at her. But no sooner was Ammavaru tied to the pillar than it became quite cool and the beaks of the crows dropped off. Seeing this, the nine worshippers of Śiva declared that the goddess was a powerful deity, and determined to strike her all together on one side. But their uplifted arms remained fixed in the air and they could not move them. Śiva then ordered Ammavaru to be tied to the feet of an elephant and dragged through the streets of the town; but as soon as she was tied to his feet, the elephant became stiff and stood motionless as a pillar. Then Śiva said that she must be thrown on to a frying-pan and fried like grain; so they took her up and threw her on to red-hot plates of glass, which at once became cool as water. Ammavaru grew wild with anger at this treatment, and, whirling round and round, became huge as a mountain, and then once more turned into a parrot, and addressed Śiva thus: "O Śiva! You failed to recognize me, but you will soon see my power. O rajas and princes! Now at last will you worship me?" The rajas and princes all cried out, "O Ammavaru! We will not worship a female deity; we will not lift our hands and salute a goddess; we will not chant any other name except 'Liṅga-nama-Śivāya.'[1] We will not think of you as a goddess." Ammavaru replied, "Never mind my worship. I am a daughter of Kasi-gotna. I was born in Valampuri. I was bred at South Virakambhodi. I am living at Ujjanimankālīpatnam. I was worshipped at Devagiri. I left Valampuri, and came to rule at Ujjanimankālī for a time. There are nine Śiva Nambis who used to worship me. They gave up wearing tirumani marks (the religious mark of the Vaishṇavites on their foreheads) and took to sacred ashes (one of the Śivaite marks). They are now

[1] See p. 132 n. 3.

worshipping Śiva in Pañchaliṅgala. Bring them to me, and I will leave your town." The nine rajas replied that they would do nothing of the kind. Then Ammavaru in her wrath threatened to destroy the town. Śiva declared that under no circumstances should she be worshipped as a goddess, and that she might do her worst. Then Ammavaru did her worst and greatly troubled the people. From east to west crows flew over the town, in vast flocks. A strong wind arose, and there was a storm of rain that lasted seven gadiyas (a gadi = 24 minutes). The people caught colds, coughs, and fevers, small-pox, and other epidemics spread rapidly; horses, elephants, and camels were afflicted with disease; pregnant women suffered severe pains; babies could not take their mothers' milk. For these seven gadiyas the town suffered terribly. All the gardens were destroyed, all flowers and plants were destroyed by white ants, all leaves by insects and bugs; all the wells and tanks were dried up. The dead bodies, heaped upon carts, were carried out by the northern gate to the burning ghat, five princesses swooned, and at last the nine rajas repented and began to abuse Śiva: "Before the moon shines, may your throne become red-hot! May your matted hair, wet with Ganges water,[1] become red with blood! May your fortress of Pañchaliṅga take fire and burn! May your pot break into pieces! May your necklace snap asunder! May your cane, held by your son, split in the middle! May you lose the Gaṅgā on your head! May your gold and silver emblems be bathed in blood!" Śiva does not seem to have been a bit dismayed at this dreadful curse. He went to the gates of Devagiri, sat upon a golden chair and brought back to life all the corpses, marked with the sacred ashes that were being taken out through the northern gate. The other corpses he left to their fate. Ammavaru then began to think that Śiva must indeed be great, but determined to

[1] Śiva, as the great ascetic, wears his hair matted, and the river Ganges falls down upon his head from heaven.

put him to another test. She created a field of sacred plants, and made the plants assume the form of human beings. Plucking some of these, she tied them together, put them on a car and sent them to Śiva. The god threw some sacred ashes on the car, touched it with his cane, and all the stalks became living men, chanting "Hara, Hara,"[1] *i.e.* Destroyer. When they asked for food, they were told that they might wander over the country, and would then get food in the shape of offerings and sacrifices. Ammavaru then went off with all her drums and instruments to Kunthalasaman, the town of Brahmā, where she hoped to find three kings worshipping her. They all received her kindly, treated her with great respect and worshipped her. Satisfied and consoled with this, she returned to her own town of Ujjanimankālī. From there she once more went up to Devagiri as an old woman, about a hundred years of age, with fruit for sale, and, entering the town without hindrance, began to sell fruits and flowers. The rajas asked their price, and she said she would sell the flowers for their weight in gold, and by this means took away all the wealth of the town, while the nine kings were doing pūjā to Śiva. Then the nine kings came to the town of Aṅkalathavatha (another name for Ammavaru) riding on clouds, to steal flowers from her garden. As they were plucking the flowers, Ammavaru seized them, took them off to an open space, where she had erected stables of gold, silver and diamonds, and impaled them in such a way that their blood could not curdle and no flies could touch them. She then placed her steed, the jackal, to guard the corpses, and then vanquished her enemies.

I have given the story almost exactly as it is told in the palm-leaf manuscript that was lent me to have copied. It is a weird rambling piece of mythology; but its interest lies in the light that it throws upon an obscure page in the history of religious life in India. We can see, beneath all its absurdity and extravagance,

[1] An epithet of Śiva.

the rise of a new form of religion side by side with the older cults of the village deities, the dislike that was felt by the upper classes for the worship of female deities, the struggle that took place between the old religion and the new, the varying phases of the conflict, the way in which disease and famine drove the masses back to the worship of their older deities, and then the drawn battle, as Śiva asserted his power and Ammavaru vanquished her enemies, and both continued to receive the worship of the people.

CHAPTER VIII

PROBABLE ORIGIN OF THE WORSHIP OF VILLAGE GODS

THE account given above of the rites and ceremonies connected with the worship of the village deities in South India does not pretend to be an exhaustive one. It would require many bulky volumes to enumerate the countless varieties of local use and custom prevailing in the different villages, and the result would be wearisome in the extreme; but enough has been said, I think, to give a fair idea of the general nature and character of this phase of Hinduism, and to form a basis of comparison, on the one hand, between the cult of the village deities and the Brāhmanical cults of Vishṇu and Śiva, and, on the other hand, between the cults of village deities existing among the Telugus, Canarese, and Tamils; and, at any rate, this brief sketch of the religion of about 80 per cent. of the Hindu population of South India may serve to dispel the idea that the people of India are, as a body, a race of philosophers, or that what is vaguely termed Hinduism is a system of refined philosophy in the purity of its morality and subtlety of its doctrines. Religious philosophy, undoubtedly, has played a great part in the development of the higher thought of the Indian people; but in South India, at any rate, the outlook of about 80 per cent. of the population on the visible world in which they live, and the invisible world which borders closely upon it, and their ideas about God and religion are represented, not by Hindu philosophy, but by the worship of their grāma-devatās.

Considerable caution must be used in drawing conclusions from the striking resemblances between the ceremonies observed in the worship of village deities among the Telugus, Canarese, and Tamils, as the value of all evidence of this kind is largely discounted by the unifying influence of the great Vijayanagar empire. For about 250 years, from A.D. 1326 to A.D. 1565, the whole of South India was united under this great empire, which had its capital on the Tungabhadra River, and formed the main bulwark of Hinduism against the advance of the Muhammadans. The capital itself was of vast extent, and gathered together men and women of all races from every part of South India. It must have formed, therefore, a great centre for the fusion of different ideas and customs; and, when the City of Vijayanagar was captured and rased to the ground by the Muhammadans in A.D. 1565, Tamils, Telugus, and Canarese may well have carried home with them many new ideas and customs borrowed from one another. We cannot assume, therefore, that, because a custom is widespread in the Tamil, Telugu, or Canarese country now, it was necessarily widespread before the foundation of the Vijayanagar empire. Allowing, however, for this possible borrowing of religious rites and ceremonies, the resemblances between the rites in all three countries are very striking. Such a curious ceremony as that of cutting off the right fore-leg and putting it into the mouth of the victim, which is found to exist all over the three countries in various villages and towns, might possibly have been borrowed; but the general resemblance in type, which underlies all local differences of custom, can hardly have been due to this cause, and the general impression left by a study of the various festivals and sacrifices in the three countries would be, I think, that they all belong to a common system and had a common origin.

In the same way caution is needed in drawing conclusions from the resemblances between the worship of the village deities and the Brāhmanical cults of Vishṇu and Śiva. The two systems of religion have existed side by side in the towns and villages for many centuries, and the same people have largely taken part in both. Naturally, therefore, they have borrowed freely from one another. In the Tamil country the influence of Brāhmanism on the cult of the village deities is very noticeable, and it is more than probable that many ceremonies, which originally belonged to the village deities, have been adopted by the Brāhman priests. No conclusions, therefore, can safely be drawn from the folklore, which represents various village goddesses as, in some way, connected with Śiva. It is quite possible that stories of this kind are simply due to a desire to connect the less dignified village deities with what was regarded as the higher form of worship controlled by the Brāhmans. On the other hand, the points of difference between the worship of the village deities and that of Śiva and Vishṇu, which have been noted in the introduction, are very strongly marked, and clearly indicate that the two systems of religion are quite distinct. The village goddesses are purely local deities, inflicting or warding off diseases and other calamities. They seem never to be regarded as having any relation to the world as a whole, and their worship is the religion of ignorant and uncivilized people, whose thoughts do not travel beyond their own surroundings and personal needs; while Śiva and Vishṇu represent a philosophic conception of great forces at work in the universe, forces of destruction and preservation, and their worship is a religion that could only have originated among men accustomed to philosophic speculation. They may have borrowed many ideas, customs, and ceremonies from the more primitive religion of the villages; but the foundation and motive of the whole system are to be sought in the brain of the philosopher rather than in the fears and superstitions of uneducated villagers. At the same time, it is also true that morally the Brāhmanical system has sunk to lower depths than have been reached by the cruder religion of the village people. The worship of the village deities contains much that is physically repulsive. The details of a buffalo sacrifice are horrid to read about, and still worse to witness, and the sight of a pūjārī parading the streets with the entrails of a lamb round his neck and its liver in his mouth would be to us disgusting; and, doubtless, there are much drunkenness and immorality connected with the village festivals; while the whole system of religion is prompted by fear and superstition, and seems almost entirely lacking in anything like a sense of sin or feelings of gratitude towards a higher spiritual Power. But still, it is also true that, setting aside a few local customs in the worship of the village deities, there is nothing in the system itself which is quite so morally degrading and repulsive as the Liṅgam worship of the Śivaites, or the marriage of girls to the god and their consequent dedication to a life of prostitution among the Vaishṇavites. If the worship of Śiva and Vishṇu has risen to greater heights, it has also sunk to lower moral depths than the less intellectual and less aesthetic worship of the grāma-devatās.

What the origin of the village deities and their worship may have been, it is difficult to say. The system, as it now exists, combines many different ideas and customs, and has probably resulted from the fusion of various forms of religion. In the Tamil country there are many features in the worship of the village deities, which, obviously, have been adopted from Brāhmanism, *e.g.* the elaborate washing of the images, and the growing aversion to animal sacrifices. So in Mysore, there are traces of sun-worship in the cult of Bisal-Mari; and there are many features in the system everywhere, which seem to be borrowed from the worship, or rather propitiation, of the spirits of the departed. But the system as a whole is redolent of the soil, and evidently belongs to a pastoral and agricultural community. The village is the centre round which the system revolves, and the protection of the villagers the object for which it exists. At the same time, it is quite possible that the ultimate origin of many of the rites and ceremonies may be traced further back to a nomadic stage of society. Most of them have now entirely lost their meaning, and, when the people are asked what a particular ceremony means or what its object is, their usual reply is simply "It is mamul," *i.e.* custom; and there are many details of the sacrifices, which seem strangely inconsistent with the general idea and theory of the worship which now prevails. The one object of all the worship and sacrifices now is to propitiate various spirits, good and evil. And this is done by means of gifts, which, it is supposed, the spirits like, or by ceremonies, which will please them. Some of the spirits are supposed to delight in bloodshed, so animals are killed in their presence, and sometimes even the blood is given them to drink; or blood and rice are sprinkled over the fields and streets, or thrown up in the air for them to eat. To the less refined goddesses or to the coarser male attendants, like Madurai-Vīran, arrack, toddy, and cheroots are freely offered, because it is assumed that these gifts will rejoice their hearts and propitiate them. But a great deal of the ritual and many of the most striking ceremonies are quite inconsistent with this gift-theory of sacrifice and the idea of propitiation, which is now assumed to be the one motive and purpose of the festivals. For instance, one of the main features of the animal sacrifices is the varied applications of the blood of the victims. Sometimes the blood is applied to the bodies of the worshippers themselves, to their foreheads and breasts; sometimes it is sprinkled on the lintel and door-posts of the shrine, sometimes on the houses or cattle, sometimes on the boundary-stones, sometimes it is mixed with rice and scattered over the streets, or sprinkled all round the boundaries of the village lands. But what possible meaning could these various uses of the blood have according to the gift-theory of sacrifice? On this theory it would be intelligible why it should be presented, as is sometimes done, at the shrine of the deity, or even drunk, as at Trichinopoly, by the pūjārī, who represents the goddess; but of these other uses of the blood the gift-theory seems to furnish no adequate explanation. Or again, what possible meaning could the gift-theory suggest for the widespread custom of putting the entrails round the neck of the pūjārī and the liver in his mouth? It is not probable that such a custom as this originated without some reason or idea at the back of it; but on the gift-theory it seems absolutely meaningless.

Or again, another leading feature of the worship is the sacrificial feast in various forms. Sometimes the feast takes place on the spot, in the compound of the shrine; more often the carcass is taken home by the offerer for a feast in his own house. Sometimes it is a formal and ceremonious act, as in certain villages of the Telugu country, where five little Mālā boys, called Siddhalu, or innocents, are fed with the flesh of the victim under cover of a large cloth, to keep off evil spirits or the evil eye. Here, again, the gift-theory seems quite inconsistent with the whole idea of the sacrificial feast. The explanation often given, that the goddess consumes the essence or spirit (*Saram* or *Avi*) of the gifts, while the worshippers take the material substance, is perhaps in accordance with the animistic idea found in other countries that, even for men, the important thing in their food is the soul-stuff it contains rather than the outward, material part of it. But in any case this would still leave unexplained the fact that the eating of the flesh by the worshippers is in many cases regarded as a religious act and as an important part of the sacrifice, like the feast on the victims offered in the peace offerings under the Jewish law. On the other hand, the sacrificial feast finds a natural and ready explanation, if we assume that the system originated in the desire for communion with the spirit world and not in the idea of propitiation.

Herr Warneck when describing the Animism of the Battaks of Sumatra in his book, *The Living Forces of the Gospel*, points out that most of the ceremonies connected with heathen sacrifices and a large number of heathen superstitions generally have their origin in the fundamental idea underlying all animistic religions, that not only living creatures and organisms but even lifeless things share in a universal soul or a soul-stuff that pervades everything in the world. "The vital question for the Animist," he says, "is how to place his own soul in relation to the souls surrounding him, and to their powers, which are partly injurious and and partly useful, with as little danger and as much advantage to himself as possible. What must I do to protect and enrich my soul? That is the cardinal question of the animistic catechism." The main object of eating the flesh of an animal, therefore, is to absorb this soul-stuff and appropriate the special virtue which belongs to the animal. "The flesh of an animal that is eaten produces an effect on man corresponding to the animal in question. The flesh of the stag gives nimbleness. Gamecocks are made to devour centipedes in order to assimilate their fierceness. Javanese thieves carry with them crow-bones to be as clever at stealing as crows." And Herr Warneck is probably right in thinking that this is the explanation of Cannibalism. It is not an act of ferocity or revenge, still less of epicureanism, since the Battaks dislike human flesh so much that it nearly makes them sick; but "it is supposed that in eating a man's flesh the eater appropriates the other's soul." And in accordance with this idea those parts of the body in which the soul-power is supposed to be concentrated, the liver, the palms of the hands, the sinews and the flesh of the head are specially prized. To the same idea we may trace the horrid custom of drinking the blood of victims offered in sacrifice, which is so common in South India, and the various uses of the blood described in Chapter III. "The soul-stuff," says Herr Warneck, "has special vigour in the blood," and it is repeatedly stated in the Jewish law with reference to the sacrificial victims that "the blood is the life."

It can readily be seen how easily in primitive times these animistic ideas gave rise to that particular form of Animism, which is generally known as Totemism. In the nomadic stage society consists of tribes or clans, the members of which are akin to one another, or, at any rate, are assumed to be united by ties of blood relationship. All the members of the clan, then, are blood relations, and are bound together, as members of one family, for mutual help and protection. The normal attitude of every clan towards other clans is one of suspicion, hostility and war, and this constant pressure of hostile clans compels each individual clan, not only to maintain its unity and brotherhood, but, if possible, to enlarge its limits and add to its numbers. It becomes possible to do this by a convenient extension of the idea of blood relationship. If a man is not one of the clan by birth, he can be made one by, in some way, being made a partaker of its blood. In his *Introduction to the History of Religion*, Mr. Jevons quotes several instances of this from different parts of the world, in both ancient and modern times. The following examples from Africa will suffice to illustrate the custom:—

> "The exchange of blood is often practised amongst the blacks of Africa, as a token of alliance and friendship. The Mambettu people, after having inflicted small wounds upon each others' arms, reciprocally suck the blood, which flows from the incision. In the Unyora country the parties dip two coffee berries into the blood, and eat them. Amongst the Sandeh the proceedings are not so repulsive; the operator, armed with two short knives, inoculates the blood of one person into the wound of another. The exact manner in which this last operation is performed is described by Mr. Ward, who himself submitted to it." After noting that blood brotherhood is a form of cementing friendship and a guarantee of good faith, popular with all the Upper Congo tribes, he proceeds: "An incision was made in both our right arms, in the outer muscular swelling just below the elbow, and as the blood flowed in a tiny stream, the charm-doctor sprinkled powdered chalk and potash on the wounds, delivering the while, in rapid tones, an appeal to us to maintain unbroken the sanctity of the contract, and then our arms being rubbed together, so that the flowing blood intermingled, we were declared to be brothers of one blood, whose interest henceforth should be united as our blood now was."

These examples will suffice to illustrate the widespread idea that the actual drinking or application of the blood of a clan will create a blood-relationship and alliance among men, who are not actually members of the same family. But the human clan in its struggle for existence found itself surrounded, not only by other human clans, but also by various tribes of animals, which it looked upon as analogous to the clans of men; and it desired to strengthen its position by an alliance with one or another of these animal clans, which, for some reason, impressed itself upon its imagination as animated by some supernatural power. The animal clan then became what is now called the totem of the human clan; and the spirit that was supposed to animate the totem clan became, in a certain sense, an object of worship. One great purpose of the sacrifice, then, was to cement and strengthen the alliance between the human clan and the animal clan; and the way in which this was done was through some application of the blood of the totem, or by, in some way, coming into contact with that which was specially connected with its life, or by partaking of its flesh. The object, then, of killing a member of the totem tribe becomes clear. Under ordinary circumstances it would be absolutely forbidden, and regarded as the murder of a kinsman; but on special occasions it was solemnly done in order to shed the blood and partake of the flesh, and so strengthen the alliance. The blood is regarded as the life, and when the blood of a member of the totem tribe of animals was shed, the life of the totem was brought to the spot where it was needed, and the blood could be applied to the worshippers as a bond of union, and then the union could be still further cemented by the feast upon the flesh, by which the spirit of the totem was absorbed and assimilated by its human kinsmen. The object of the animal sacrifice, therefore, was not in any sense to offer a gift, but to obtain communion with the totem-spirit.

Now, if we apply this theory of sacrifice to the sacrifices offered to the village deities in South India, we see that the main ceremonies connected with them at once become intelligible; the various modes of sprinkling and applying the blood, and the different forms of the sacrificial feast were all originally intended to promote communion with the spirit that was worshipped. In the same way, even such a ceremony as the wearing of the entrails round the neck, and putting the liver in the mouth, acquires an intelligible meaning and purpose. The liver and entrails are naturally connected with the life of the animal, and the motive of this repulsive ceremony would seem to be an intense desire to obtain as close communion as possible with the object of worship by wearing those parts of its body that are specially connected with its life. So, too, this theory explains why the animal sacrificed is so often treated as an object of worship. In the case of the buffalo sacrifices in the Telugu country, as we have seen, the buffalo is paraded through the village, decked with garlands and smeared with turmeric and kunkuma, and then, as it passes by the houses, people come out and pour water on its feet, and worship it. But why should this be done if the animal sacrificed is regarded as only a gift to the goddess? When, however, we realize that the animal sacrificed was not originally regarded as a gift, but as a member of the totem tribe and the representative of the spirit to be worshipped, the whole ceremony becomes full of meaning.

Then, again, this theory of the origin of sacrifice supplies a very plausible and intelligible explanation of the origin of the use of stones and images to represent the village deities in India. At first sight it seems a complete mystery why a common ordinary stone should be regarded as representing a god or goddess. Most of the stones used for this purpose in South Indian villages have absolutely nothing that is peculiar or distinctive about them. Often they are simply stone pillars of varying heights, and a large number are only small, conical stones, not more than six or seven inches high. Some, again, are flat slabs with figures carved on them in bas-relief and others are regular images. The images and carved bas-reliefs we can understand; but how could these ordinary stones and stone-pillars have ever come to be regarded as the representatives of spiritual beings? The theory of sacrifice connected with totemism supplies, at any rate, a possible and intelligible explanation. The totem animal was killed in order to shed the blood, and so secure the presence of the totem deity at a particular spot, which then became sacred or Taboo. To violate it would be a grievous offence. Accordingly the spot was marked by a simple heap of stones, or by an upright stone pillar, which would perhaps be sprinkled with the blood. Then, as totemism gradually died out and gave place to higher religious ideas and anthropomorphic conceptions of deity, the old totemistic conception of sacrifice became obscured, and the animal that was killed was regarded no longer as the representative of the object of worship, but as a gift to the deity. At the same time the sanctity of the spot became associated with the stones, originally set up to mark the place of sacrifice, and so in time the stone pillar itself became sacred, and came to be treated as the symbol of the deity to whom the sacrifice was offered, while the heap of stones developed into the sacred altar. We can probably trace one stage of this process of evolution in the ideas now connected with the boundary-stone, ellai-kal. No doubt it was once simply a stone placed to mark the spot, on the boundary of the village lands, where the sacrifice was offered. Then the stone became sacred, and the idea grew up that it was inhabited by the spirit who was worshipped. There, however, the process of evolution stopped, and the stone is not now regarded, like the other stones, as representing the deity, but simply as her abode.

Probably the other stones were once regarded in exactly the same light, and then advanced a step further and became representatives of the deities worshipped. The next step, to the carved human figures, whether bas-reliefs or complete images, would be easy and natural, when once the deity had been conceived no longer as the spirit of a whole species of animals, but as akin to human beings.

When this change in religious ideas took place must, of course, be a matter of conjecture, but it probably coincided with the change from the nomadic to the settled pastoral and agricultural life, when the wandering clan developed into the village community, and the superiority of man to the lower animals had been definitely established.

Similarly, it is possible that the connexion between the growth of agriculture and the origin of village communities and so also of village deities, may account for the fact that the village deities of South India are almost always females.

All over the world the earth spirit is regarded as female and the presiding deities of agriculture are mainly goddesses, because the idea of fertility and reproduction is connected with women. When, therefore, a nomadic pastoral clan settled down to an agricultural life in villages, they would naturally worship the earth-spirits of the village lands as goddesses rather than as gods.

The fact, too, that agriculture among primitive races was the business of women rather than of men, as it is among savage races at the present day, probably led to the village goddesses being at first worshipped by the women rather than by the men. One trace of this is still found in the custom of the Mālā pūjārī, who is a man, dressing up as a woman when he sits in the cart with the animals impaled alive all around him, and is dragged in procession through the village,[1] as well as in the prominent part taken by women in some places in the waving of the āratī.[2]

These theories as to the origin of the village deities, of idolatry and of animal sacrifice in South India, can, of course, be regarded only as hypotheses. But, when we consider that the totemistic theory is able to furnish a plausible explanation of the crude form of idolatry which exists in many villages, and of many features in the sacrificial rites, which seem quite inconsistent with the existing ideas of sacrifice, we see that there is sufficient evidence to justify its adoption

[1] See above, p. 58. [2] See above, p. 39.

as a working hypothesis. And there can be no doubt that the ceremonial observed in these sacrifices gives very substantial support to the theory, that the original idea of sacrifice was not that of a gift to the deity but communion with a supernatural power. And, if that is true, then we may see, even in these primitive rites, a foreshadowing of far higher forms of religious belief and practice. The mysterious efficacy attributed to the sprinking of the blood might almost be regarded as an unconscious prophecy of the Christian doctrine of the Atonement, while the whole ritual of the sacrifices, even in its crudest and most revolting forms, bears witness to that instinctive craving after communion with God, which finds its highest expression and satisfaction in the sacramental system of the Christian Church.

CHAPTER IX

SOCIAL, MORAL, AND RELIGIOUS INFLUENCE OF THE SYSTEM

THE results of this system of religion might at first seem to be wholly degrading intellectually, morally, and spiritually. It appears on the surface to be a religion of fear and superstition, finding its outward expression in mean, ugly symbols, and in forms of worship that are to a very large extent disgusting and even immoral. The account of a village festival in the Telugu country reads like mere midsummer madness; many of the rites in which animals are impaled or buried alive are revolting in their cruelty; and the animal sacrifices with their crude butchery and coarse bloodshed bear witness to a low and unworthy conception of deity. Whatever may have been the origin of these animal sacrifices in prehistoric times, they are now regarded by the worshippers simply as a means of appeasing the deity's wrath by satisfying her lust for blood. In the ancient Jewish sacrifices there may have been the same amount of bloodshed and butchery, when on such an occasion as the dedication of the Temple at Jerusalem "King Solomon offered a sacrifice of twenty and two thousand oxen and a hundred and twenty thousand sheep," but the Jewish sacrifices symbolized great moral and spiritual truths; the victim represented the worshipper, the killing of the animal and the offering of the blood expressed the consecration of the worshipper's own life to God; in the sin offering and the peace offering the presentation of the blood and the feast on the flesh were symbolical of penitence for sin and communion with God. But in the sacrifices to the village deities in India at the present day there are no traces of those higher ideas in the minds of the worshippers. There is no penitence for sin, no thought of the consecration of human life to a just and holy God, but simply the desire to appease the ill-temper of a vengeful spirit by an offering of blood. And even in unbloody offerings of fruit, camphor, and incense to the more refined and respectable of the goddesses, who are supposed to be shocked by the sight of blood, the idea of sacrifice does not rise above the conception of a propitiatory gift. It is the kind of offering that is made to the local policeman or a tyrannical government official to secure his favour. And in almost all the festivals held in honour of the village deities there is a wild orgiastic excitement, and often a sad amount of drunkenness and immorality that is most degrading. So, too, there is nothing morally elevating in the conception formed of the characters of the deities themselves. They have not even the grandeur of such a deity as Śiva. Śiva may be terrible and cruel, but at any rate there is something grand and majestic about him: he represents a world-force; he is an interpretation of the universe and the embodiment of a philosophy. But the village deity is nothing more than a petty local spirit, tyrannizing over or protecting a small hamlet, occasionally venting her spite or her ill-temper on a handful of poor villagers. She inspires fear because of her power to do grievous harm by inflicting diseases and injuries on man and beast when she is offended, but she has no relation to the universe or even to the world: she is the product of fear untouched by philosophic reflection; so she does not draw out any feelings of wonder and admiration, still less of love and gratitude, nor does she lead her worshippers on to any higher ideals of morality.

Taking the system, therefore, as a whole, as it exists at the present day, we can only condemn it from a moral and religious point of view as a debasing superstition, and the only attitude which the Christian Church can possibly take towards it as a working system is one of uncompromising hostility, the same attitude that the Jewish prophets of old took to the local Semitic cults in Palestine with all their idolatrous and immoral associations. In the writings of Hindu philosophers and poets there are many noble and inspiring thoughts, but there is nothing in the vast jungle of beliefs and practices that have grown up during the course of ages around the worship of the village deities that the Christian Church could wish to preserve. The first step towards any religious progress in the villages of South India is to cut down this jungle of beliefs and practices, rites and ceremonies, and clear the ground for the teaching and worship of the Christian Church. When the Outcastes of a village in the Telugu country become Christians, they very often level the shrine of their local deity to the ground and build a Christian prayer-house on the site. That expresses the general attitude of Christianity to the whole system.

At the same time we must not allow the corruptions of the system at the present day, with all its debasing rites and its low and petty views of the deity, to blind us to its social and religious value in past ages, or to the deeper spiritual feelings and instincts which it has feebly striven to express. In the first place, the worship of the village deities has maintained a silent protest on behalf of religious and social equality. Feeble and ineffective as the protest may be, still it is a protest that is not without its value. In the worship of the village deities there is no priestly caste. The Brāhman is nowhere; the pūjāris may belong to any caste; the leading part in the buffalo sacrifices is nearly always taken by the Outcastes; the folklore of the village deities and the songs chanted at the sacrifices give hints of a time when the Outcastes aspired to equality with the Brāhmans; and the large number of people from the different Śūdra castes who take part in the sacrifices form a striking witness to what we should call in the Christian Church the priesthood of the laity. It is a feeble flickering light shining in a dark place, like the witness borne to the equality and brotherhood of man at the temple of Jagannath in Orissa, where all castes, including the Brāhmans, eat together. Still the witness has been maintained through the long centuries of caste tyranny, and perhaps it has had more influence than we imagine in keeping alive in the hearts of the depressed classes some slight feeling of self-respect and a sense of their own worth in the community. It is something to be proud of that when the terrible calamity of cholera or small-pox threatens the life of the village, the calamity cannot be averted without their help. If they cannot feel that they are respected, the next best thing is to feel that in times of trouble they are needed.

Then, in the second place, deep down in the system, buried beneath a mass of traditional rites that have lost their meaning, there is still the instinctive craving of the human heart for communion with God. This instinctive feeling after God has indeed been degraded by unworthy and petty ideas of the spiritual world; it has been distorted by fear and superstition; it has found expression in weird and horrid forms; but still, in spite of all corruptions and distortions, we can discern in it, not merely a belief in a spirit world, but a desire to come into personal communion with spiritual beings. In the previous chapter it has been shown that the original idea underlying the system of animal sacrifice was that of communion rather than that of propitiation; and, though at the present day propitiation by acceptable gifts is undoubtedly the dominant idea in these sacrifices and offerings, still the idea of communion is not wholly lost. The pūjārī is often regarded as possessed and inspired by the deity, and the sprinkling of the blood of the victim on the houses, the fields and the persons of the worshippers is regarded as a means of securing the presence and protection of the deity. While, therefore, the methods of communion are all wrong, and the conception of the deity with whom communion is sought is hopelessly inadequate and perverted, still, in the simple desire for communion with a deity of some sort, there is a germ and root of true religious feeling which craves for expression. It is pathetic to notice how real is the desire among many of the more religious men and women in the villages, even among the depressed classes, to see God. I have often met with and heard of men who have spent what are for them large sums of money, and undergone much hardship, to satisfy this desire. We must not undervalue this rudimentary religious feeling; and if, in the worship of the village deities, it has for many centuries been feeding on carrion, perhaps it is better for it to feed on carrion than to die of starvation.

Then, again, the belief in the village deities has undoubtedly fostered an attitude of mind towards the spiritual world which is to a certain degree a preparation for the Gospel. It has made men feel a sense of dependence on spiritual beings. The mental attitude of the ordinary villager is the very antithesis of materialism or agnoticism. He has a very vivid belief that the world in which he lives is surrounded by unseen spiritual beings, and in all times of trouble he feels intensely his dependence on his village deity for help and protection. And even where the village deity is conceived of as an ill-tempered, revengeful being, the fear which she inspires is not a bad preparation for a belief in a God of love. The experience of most evangelists among the Outcastes of South India would be, I think, that their fear of evil spirits is one reason why the doctrine of an omnipotent God of infinite love appeals to them with so much force. It makes them realize their need of help. It does for them what the fear of powerful and malicious enemies did for the Jewish people of old. The Jewish Psalms show how closely the need of protection from powerful enemies was bound up with the deepest religious feelings of the chosen people. The need of protection against evil spirits is playing a similar part in the religious development of the villagers of South India.

The Christian Church thus brings to the villagers,

and especially to the Outcastes, three great truths which their belief in the village deities specially prepares them to accept:

(*a*) First, the truth of the existence of an omnipotent God of infinite love, the creator and the ruler of the universe, and the Father of all mankind, a truth which stands out in vivid and startling contrast to their belief in a multitude of evil or ill-tempered spirits always ready to do them grievous harm, with no superior power to control them.

(*b*) Second, the truth of the universal redemption from sin and the great gift of direct, personal access to an almighty, all-loving God through Jesus Christ. This truth stands in equally striking contrast to the poor and miserable communion with a petty local deity offered through the blood of their animal sacrifices. To compare great things with small, it is as though a poor villager suffering from the persecution of a petty local official were suddenly told that he had free right of access to the kind and powerful collector of the district. The good news of free access to God is a real Gospel of freedom.

(*c*) And thirdly, there is the great truth of the equality of all men in God's sight and the universal brotherhood of man. It is a truth very dimly foreshadowed in the rites of their primitive cult; but in the Christian Church it stands out as the very essence of the Gospel message. And it is a truth that makes a powerful appeal to the hearts of the downtrodden and depressed.

Thus, while the cult of the village deities provides little foundation of belief or practice on which the Christian Church can build; on the other hand it has kept alive a sense of deep spiritual needs, which Christianity alone can satisfy. It certainly brings religion down into the every-day life of the people. The ordinary villager of South India does nothing without offering prayer to the village deity, while the shrines and symbols that are scattered all over the countryside keep constantly before his mind the existence of a spiritual world. However poor and degraded his ideas of deity may be, at any rate they are to him a profound reality, and this sense of the reality and importance of the spiritual world is not a bad foundation for the Christian Church to build upon.

APPENDIX I

On the Ceremony of the Opening of the Mouth in the Funeral Rites of Ancient Egypt

There is an interesting parallel to the practice of cutting off the right foreleg and putting it in the mouth of the buffalo (described on page 51) in the ancient funeral ceremonies connected with the cult of Osiris in Egypt. The legend ran that, after Osiris had been murdered by his brother Set, his son Horus sought out his body, in order to raise it to life; and, when he found it, he untied the bandages so that Osiris might move his limbs and rise up. Under the direction of Thoth, Horus recited a series of formulas, as he presented offerings to Osiris; and he and his sons and Anubis performed the ceremonies which opened the mouth and nostrils, and the eyes and ears of Osiris. This opening of the mouth was one of the regular funeral rites in ancient Egypt.

There is a book found in tombs called the Book of the Opening of the Mouth; and in a British Museum bulletin, entitled *The Book of the Dead*, written by Mr. E. A. Wallis Budge, it is said that, on the upper margins of the insides of coffins, there are frequently given two or more rows of coloured drawings of the offerings which under the fifth dynasty were presented to the deceased or his statue during the celebration of the service of "Opening the Mouth." In one of the illustrations the ceremony of Opening the Mouth is shown as being performed on the mummy of a royal scribe. In the picture there is a calf walking in front of its mother with its left foreleg cut off, and in front of the calf are two slaves, one with the heart of the deceased in his hand, and the other holding the left foreleg of the calf, which is apparently being placed upon a table. It is not clear what part the foreleg plays in the ceremony of the "Opening of the Mouth," but there is an obvious resemblance between this ancient ceremony in Egypt and the widespread custom in South India mentioned above. The Egyptian ceremony suggests that one object of putting the foreleg in the mouth in the case of sacrifices in India is to keep it open and enable the spirit of the animal to go in and out.

We give in Plate XVIII a photograph of a buffalo sacrifice carried out by the servants of Dr. Hunt of Secunderabad. The scene is the garage in which his motor bicycle stands. Round it the servants have grouped his sword, the gardener's shears, a baby's chair, a tea-kettle, etc., and to these the sacrifice was made. In the right foreground lies the body of the buffalo, to the left its head with the right foreleg in its mouth, while between the head and the bicycle may be seen a bottle of liquor and various other offerings.

APPENDIX II

On the Use of Iron to Drive Away Evil Spirits

A curious custom connected with the worship of Mariamma was brought to my notice by Dr. Hunt of Secunderabad. An Indian friend of his came across it in a village of the Bellary district in the Telugu country. The villagers hold a festival in honour of the goddess Mariamma every year and offer the usual sacrifices. In 1917 there was a very severe epidemic of influenza in the district; so a special festival was held to appease the wrath of the goddess. A wooden bust of her was made with arms akimbo and sacrifices were duly offered to it. Thousands of people came from neighbouring villages for the occasion, to do pūjā and make their offerings. On the following night the image was placed on a small wooden cart about three feet high, and taken in procession to a place outside the village. The head of each family then came and drove an iron nail into the image, till it was dotted all over with nails. A goat was then sacrificed, and the blood sprinkled over the goddess; after which the image and the cart were covered over with a red cloth and left in the field. A rough drawing of the nail-filled image is reproduced in Plate XVIII. The explanation of this ceremony given by the villagers themselves was that the nails were driven in to the goddess to attract her attention and induce her to be kind to each family and protect them against the disease. It seems an odd way of doing it; and probably the real meaning of the ceremony in prehistoric times was somewhat different. It is a very old and wide-spread idea that malignant spirits are afraid of iron; and it is possible that the hammering of the nails into the goddess was originally intended to put the fear of iron into her and drive out of her the evil temper. The villagers do not now connect the practice with black magic (*bhanamati*); but the original idea may have been in some way connected with it. But whatever the origin, it throws an interesting light on the driving of nails into the famous Hindenburg statue in Berlin during the war. Evidently this is a survival of an old pagan custom dating back to a remote antiquity.

It is a common belief among all castes in Malabar[1] that lonely places, such as cremation grounds, the sides of tanks or groves of tamarind trees, are haunted by "pisachas" or evil spirits. At about the middle of the night these evil spirits are supposed to roam about their haunts with the intention of possessing those who chance to pass their way. People who say that they have seen the demon give us to understand that it has the form of a woman, and less often of a man, while others say that its form is too fearful to describe, attesting that, if they could believe their eyes, they saw a hideous and most appalling figure towering right up to the skies. Men are much afraid to pass through such places between nine p.m. and three a.m., but feel themselves safe when they have sharp iron weapons with them. It is supposed that the devil is afraid of iron and goes away in a fright. A man versed in magic, when he has to walk through such places, draws a cabalistic figure on the earth, and inscribes on it some mystical letters. At the centre of the figure he plunges the pointed end of an iron knife or peg. Having done this, he feels quite secure from the baneful influence of evil spirits.

Sometimes a house is believed to be haunted by some of these aerial beings. When calamities come thick upon the inmates of a house, it is a certain sign that it is possessed by evil spirits. In such a case the

[1] These notes about Malabar were kindly given me by one of the assistants of the Government Museum, Madras.

exorciser is sent for. He comes and studies the situation of the house and the position of the doors and windows and so on. Having got a thorough knowledge of it, he is able to say which way the devil comes and goes. A suitable corner is selected, according to the rules of sorcery, and an iron nail is driven into the earth at that corner. The devil is bound down by such an act, and the householder feels that he has nothing more to fear from demoniacal influences.

To cast out the devil that has possessed a man or a woman, the following method is very commonly resorted to. A wooden image of the person under the power of the evil spirit is made, and a square hole made in it just above the navel. The wood selected for this purpose is, as a rule, that of the *palamaram*, *i.e. alstozia scholaris*. This is done according to the rules of magic. Then, by the recitation of certain mysterious spells, the essence of the person afflicted with the malady is transferred to the wooden image. The idea of incising a hole in the image seems to me to be to create an opening or entrance in the image through which the essence of the person can be transferred to it. There might also be another idea, that such an image should not be perfect in every part. The image is then taken to a tree that has plenty of milky juice in it and nailed on to it. The tree selected for such purposes is *palamaram*, *i.e. alstozia scholaris*, *arayalmaram*, *i.e. ficus religiosa*, or *pezhumaram*, *i.e. careya arborea*. The spirit no longer possesses the person but possesses the tree.

In the Madras Museum there are two large wooden images, over five feet high, studded all over with wooden nails. The first, a life-size rude female human figure, with feet turned backwards, carved out of the wood of *alstoria scholaris*, was washed ashore at Calicut in 1903. It probably came from the Laccadive islands, some of whose residents are famous necromancers. The figure probably represented a woman possessed by an evil spirit. By means of magic rites and the driving in of the nails, the people believed they had nailed up the spirit in the image, and then threw it into the sea. The other figure was found at Tellicherry. Arabic characters, doubtless regarded as of great magic potency, are carved all over the figures.

The use of iron to scare away evil spirits is very common among the Chamārs in North India.[1]

[1] Briggs, *The Chamārs*, 142.

GLOSSARY OF INDIAN TERMS

As only brief definitions are possible here, a reference is given in each case to the page on which the term is explained. Names of deities are not included. They may be found in the indices.

abishegām — anointing, washing, 92.
ādi—original, 133.
amma or *amman*—a feminine termination, 23.
ārati—a lamp of rice flour, 39.
arrack—a native intoxicant, 49.
Asādis—priests of the Mālās, 44.
ashṭa śakti—the eight powers of the universe, 30.
avatāra—incarnation, 24.
bali—offering, 82.
bali-harana — presentation of the offering, 63.
basava—bull or ox, 125.
basavī—a fallen woman consecrated to a deity, 45.
betel—a pepper plant, 39.
bhadrākshī—a kind of bead, 129.
boddu-rayee—navel-stone. 60.
Brāhman—the highest Hindu caste, 19.
Chakras—a section of the Outcastes, 81.
Chaṇḍāla - an Outcaste, 84.
cholam—a coarse grain, 50.
damaru — a Śivaite drum, 129 n. I.
devara kona—consecrated buffalo, 78.
devara-potu — consecrated to the goddess, 62.
dola-jātra — swing-festival, 59 n. 1.
dubakaya—a fruit, 67.
ellai-kal—boundary-stone, 33.
Gaṅgā-bhavanī—a fortified place, 129.
ganja—Indian hemp used as an intoxicant, 90.
gauda-kona—husband - buffalo, 73.
gingelly—a plant, 90.
golla—milkman, 75.
gopuram—the towered gateway of a South Indian temple, 134.
gram—lentils, 64.
grāma-devatā—village-god, 16.
Hara—destroyer, 137.
inam—rent-free land, 63.
Kaniyas—religious mendicants found in Coorg, 87.
kaṅkanam—a bracelet, 105.
kapu—a yellow wristlet, 100.
karagam—pot, 37.
karṇam—a village accountant, 44.
kavalgar—village watchman, 106.
kitchadi—a dish of flour and buttermilk, 81.
krita yuga—the golden age, 132.
krittam—a conical head-dress, 26.
Kshatriya—the second Hindu caste, 19.
kunkuma—a red paste, 50.
kunna-kannadi—eye-mirror, 29.
Kuttadis—dancers, 27.
liṅga—Śiva's phallic symbol, 72 n. 1.
Liṅgāyats—a sect who wear the liṅga, 72.

Mādigās—the lowest section of the Outcastes in the Telugu country, 28.
Mālās—a large group of Outcastes in the Telugu country, 44.
mantram—a sacred text, 92.
maranada bali—death-atonement, 88.
margosa—the neem tree, 37.
mleccha—a foreigner, 19.
muhūrtam—moment, 132.
mund—a group of huts, 61.
munsiff—a village magistrate, 57.
namaskāram—obeisance, 66.
nautch-girls—dancing girls attached to temples, 21.
Pambala—a hereditary Mālā priest, 58.
Pañchama—an Outcaste, 19.
pandal—booth, 37.
Panikas—religious mendicants, 86, 87.
Pariahs—the chief group of Outcastes in the Tamil country, 14.
pedda—great, 70.
pial—platform, 81.
prasādam—a grace-gift, 64.
pūjā—worship, 18.
pūjārī—one who conducts worship, a ministrant, 18.
puthrayāgam—a sacrifice to obtain a child, 31.
rakshatha—demon, 122.
reddy—a village magistrate, 71.
rudrāksha—a kind of berry, 129.
ryot—a small farmer, 52.
śakti—power, 29.
śāstras—the Hindu sacred books, 84.
shashṭhāṅgam—prostration, 74.
siddhalu—innocents, 52.
Śūdra—the fourth Hindu caste, 19.
śūlam—spear, 40.
tahsildar—the magistrate of a sub-division of a district, 57.
tali—a marriage disk, 27, 132.
taliāri—a village servant, 72.
tapas—austerities, 84.
tom-tom—a native drum, 38.
toti—watchman, 78.
Trimūrti—the Hindu triad, 24.
triśūla—trident, 40 n. 2.
turmeric—a dye, 48.
vāhana—vehicle, 90.
Vaiśya—the third Hindu caste, 19.
veta—sacrifice, 70.
vetty—scavenger, 56.
vīran—hero, 33.
yuga—an age, 132.
zamindar—land-owner, 57.

INDEX OF THE GODS

A. Female

B. Male

C. Stones

GEOGRAPHICAL INDEX

A. The Telugu Country: 18, 23-24, 36, 40, 43, Chap. IV.

B. The Tamil Country: 18, 19, 33, 35, 37, 38, 43, 45, 51, 61, Chap. VI.

C. The Canarese Country: 23-24, 37, 40, 43, 49, Chap. V.

D. The Nilgiris and Coorg: 61.

GENERAL INDEX